Windows® .NET Server Security Handbook

DR. CYRUS PEIKARI
SETH FOGIE

ISBN 0-13-047726-5

Prentice Hall PTR
Upper Saddle River, NJ 07458
www.phptr.com

A CIP catalog record for this book can be obtained from the Library of Congress.

Editorial/Production Supervision: *MetroVoice Publishing Services*
Senior Managing Editor: *Karen McLean*
Editorial Assistant: *Richard Winkler*
Marketing Manager: *Bryan Gambrel*
Manufacturing Manager: *Alexis Heydt-Long*
Cover Design: *Nina Scuderi*
Cover Design Direction: *Jerry Votta*
Art Director: *Gail Cocker-Bogusz*
Series Design: *Meg VanArsdale*

 © 2002 Prentice Hall PTR
A Division of Pearson Education, Inc.
Upper Saddle River, New Jersey 07458

Prentice Hall books are widely used by corporations and government agencies for
training, marketing, and resale. For information regarding corporate and government
bulk discounts please contact: Corporate and Government Sales (800) 382-3419 or
corpsales@pearsontechgroup.com

Printed in the United States of America

10   9   8   7   6   5   4   3   2   1

ISBN 0-13-0477265

Pearson Education Ltd.
Pearson Education Australia PTY Ltd.
Pearson Education Singapore, Pte. Ltd.
Pearson Education North Asia Ltd.
Pearson Education Canada, Ltd.
Pearson Educación de Mexico, S.A. de C.V.
Pearson Education—Japan
Pearson Education Malaysia, Pte. Ltd.

Part III   Windows .NET Client Security: Protecting Windows XP   87

attempts to break into your computer and gain unauthorized privileges by guessing passwords, he will be unsuccessful or will obtain only limited, guest-level access.

Moreover, the **Anonymous Logon** group is no longer a member of the **Everyone** group. A client that accesses a computer through the network without an account name, password, or domain is a member of the Anonymous Logon built-in security group. By design, in previous versions of Windows, members of the Anonymous Logon security group had access to many resources due to innate membership in the Everyone group. This was a potential security weakness, because system administrators might not realize that anonymous users were members of the Everyone group and might accidentally grant them access to resources only intended for authenticated users.

When a Windows 2000 system is upgraded to Windows .NET, resources with permission entries for the Everyone group (and not explicitly to the Anonymous Logon group) will no longer be available to anonymous users after the upgrade. However, you may wish to permit anonymous access in order to support preexisting applications that require it. In order to grant access to the Anonymous logon group, you will need to specifically add the Anonymous Logon security group and its permissions.

However, in some situations where it might be difficult to determine and modify the permission entries on resources hosted on Windows .NET Servers, you can change the default security setting under Local Computer Policy as follows:

1. Click **Start** ➤ (**Settings**) ➤ **Control Panel**.
2. Click (**Performance and Maintenance**) ➤ **Administrative Tools**.
3. Click **Local Security Policy** and open the **Security Options** folder.
4. Locate **Network access: Let Everyone permissions apply to anonymous users** and adjust the setting to **Enabled** (see Figures 2.2 and 2.3).

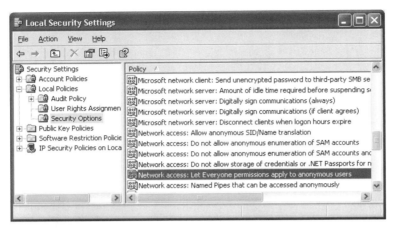

Figure 2.2
Local Security Settings window.

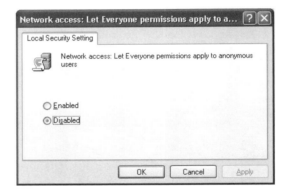

Figure 2.3
Adjusting Everyone permissions.

If this policy is enabled, the Everyone security identifier (SID) is added to the token created for anonymous connections. In this case, anonymous users are able to access any resource for which the Everyone group has been given permissions.

Blank Password Restriction

Windows .NET accounts without passwords can only be used to log on at the physical computer console. This feature was added to protect users who do not password protect their accounts. By default, accounts with blank passwords can no longer be used to log on to the computer remotely over the network or for any other logon activity except at the main physical console logon screen.

For instance, you cannot use the secondary logon service (**RunAs**) to start a program as a local user with a blank password. When the user assigns a password to their local account, this removes the restriction and allows them to log on over a network. It also permits that account to access any resources it is authorized to access, even over a network connection.

Encrypting File System and Offline Files

The Encrypting File System (EFS) of Windows .NET includes new features as well. Just as in its Windows 2000 predecessor, the new Windows .NET EFS architecture is based on public-key encryption and the Windows CryptoAPI. As before, EFS can use either the expanded Data Encryption Standard (DESX) or Triple-DES (3DES) as the encryption algorithm.

New in Windows .NET is the ability of the EFS to work with offline files and folders. Windows 2000 introduced the client-side caching functionality, now called Offline Files. Windows .NET now gives you the option to encrypt the Offline Files database.

This is an improvement over Windows 2000, where the cached files could not be encrypted. Windows .NET offers you the option of encrypting the Offline Files database to safeguard all locally cached documents from theft while at the same time providing additional security to your locally cached data. For example, you can use offline files while keeping your sensitive data secure. Also, administrators can use this feature to safeguard all locally cached documents. This feature supports the encryption and decryption of the entire offline database.

Remote Desktop

Users of previous Windows server platforms will be familiar with rudimentary remote access applications that allowed one or more remote users to connect to a server and operate it as if the user was sitting in front of the physical computer. While this technology served its purpose, it was limited. Colors were few, features were thin, and permissions were difficult to manage.

Figure 2.4
Remote Desktop Connection window.

With the release of Windows XP and .NET, Microsoft has significantly upgraded the Remote Desktop feature to the point where a remote user experiences no difference between physically sitting at the host computer and remotely operating it (see Figure 2.4). The extra features are numerous and include:

• 24 bit color display
• Streaming sound from host to client
• Auto start of programs on connection
• Optional connection of local drives and printers to remote host
• Various visual performance options

These added features alone give Windows .NET a significant advantage over its competitors and previous editions of Windows. The new remote desktop allows you to easily manage several computers with only one monitor, keyboard, mouse, and pair of speakers. In addition, remote users who need access to their files or programs can use Remote Desktop to easily connect from any client computer on the network, providing the host is running Windows XP.

Smart Card Administrative Utilities

In Windows .NET Server, utilities such as **Net.exe** and **Runas.exe** have been enabled to support Smart Card credentials. Thus, administrators can use alternate credentials to conduct routine tasks with normal user privileges while at the same time executing special administrator functions.

Windows .NET Wireless Security

802.1x—Port-Based Network Access Control

In April 2001, Microsoft announced that it would be supporting a new wireless security standard in its Windows XP and .NET Server operating systems. The new standard was designed to enhance the ease and security with which users of PCs, laptops, and handheld devices interface with a wireless Internet connection. The standard, which is known as 802.1x, was also adopted by other network equipment manufacturers including 3Com, Cisco, and Enterasys Networks; PC makers Compaq Computers, IBM, and Dell; and chipmakers Intel, Intersil, and others.

The goal of the new security standard is to fix many of the security vulnerabilities that UC–Berkeley computer scientists found in wireless networks based on the wireless standard Wi-Fi, or 802.11B. In February 2001, university researchers found holes in wireless networks that let hackers intercept or hijack transmissions.

Many of the companies adopting this standard sell wireless products that include notebook PC cards that have radio transmitters and receivers built-in. Others sell a hardware product that is affixed to ceilings or walls that can link the computers to an Internet connection. This piece of hardware, known as an "access point," can link up to a range of several hundred feet.

The new standard provides several improvements. For example, password deployment has been made easier. Previously, network administrators had to manually install a password on each laptop in order for an employee to connect to the wireless network. Those passwords, also known as passphrases, were static and thus more vulnerable. However, the new standard improves security by giving users a dynamic password each time they connect to a wireless network.

In addition, the previous technology allowed employees to connect to one access point only. Fortunately, the new standard allows a user to connect with the same password across multiple access points.

At this point, Virtual Private Networks (VPNs) still provide the best security while on a wireless network. However, the new Port-Based Network Access Control standard has provided a significant improvement over existing wireless security.

New Windows .NET Server Wireless Features

The following is a list of new Wireless features integrated into Windows .NET Server:

- Secure access to the network via IEEE 802.1X support, to support wireless LANs and Ethernet. This feature ensures that the connection to the rest of your system will be encrypted and secure from prying eyes. Read about wireless hacking in Chapter 6.

- Enables interoperable user identification, centralized authentication, and dynamic key management. This feature is important to verify that the wireless user belongs on the network. Just as cell phones can pick up random conversations, a wireless network must also deal with this potential situation.

- Builds on existing standards, especially EAP and RADIUS. This ensures that Windows .NET will work in existing wireless networks. Standardization is needed to keep everyone talking the same language.

- Can secure both wired and wireless LAN access. Windows .NET does not necessarily need a wireless network to use the security features that are built into it. Both wired and wireless networks are supported.

- Network location API (via Windows Sockets). This feature is for programmers. All it does is ensure that programs can easily tie into the wireless network via hooks preset by Windows.

- Network location tells the application to which network the machine is connected (for example, at home or work) and information about the type of network connection (speed, LAN or PPP, whether the machine is connected to the Internet, and so on). This provides applications with the capability to configure per network, for example, application proxies.

- Can be used in addition to existing APIs to provide network-aware applications. This feature, also used by programmers, will allow applications to detect network availability.
- Automatic network detection and configuration for 802.11 LANs. For the average user, setting up a wireless network may seem difficult. Windows helps this user by detecting and setting it up for them.
- Network identification and mode selection (infrastructure/ad hoc) for 802.11 LANs. In larger networks there may be more than one wireless access point. Therefore, the software must be able to detect and use the correct connection.
- Radio power management and balancing between power savings and performance. This feature turns the wireless network on when it is needed, and off when it is not, thus saving precious energy. This is especially useful for battery-powered laptops.
- Intelligent network interface selection based on speed and media type. In multimode environments, one access point may be closer or faster than another. This feature automatically selects the best one for the job.

Summary

Windows .NET Server and its client, Windows XP Pro, provide numerous security enhancements for networks of all sizes. This chapter has given a brief overview of the security features that are brand-new in Windows .NET and XP. Subsequent chapters will cover each of these topics, as well as the core security architecture of Windows .NET Server, in greater detail.

Securing Windows .NET Remote Desktop

Chapter 3

SECURING THE REMOTE DESKTOP

This chapter covers:

- Introduction to the Remote Desktop
- Installation of the Remote Desktop Connection
- Setup of the Remote Desktop Web Connection client
- Installation of the Remote Desktop Web components
- Setup of the Remote Desktop Web Connection
- Connection instructions for the Remote Desktop Web Connection
- Security issues surrounding the Remote Desktop
- Common errors that may occur when using Remote Desktop Connection

Overview

The Achilles' heel of Windows .NET Server security is its client, Windows XP Pro. Thanks to the increasing use of IPSec to provide encrypted traffic (Chapter 14), the face of network security will change drastically. As we will see later in the book, Virtual Private Networks (VPN) provide a secure tunnel for the home tele-commuter to access the internal, remote corporate network. Unfortunately, that means all an intruder has to do is hack the home user's laptop, and they also now have a secure tunnel into the enterprise! For this reason, as an administrator you should understand security on the clients that connect to your .NET Server.

Windows XP includes a new remote-control feature known as *remote desktop*, which is designed to supplant the embryonic *terminal services* feature of prior Windows operating systems. Remote desktop allows a remote user to connect to a Windows session from any computer, at any location, which is similar to Symantec's PC Anywhere or AT&T's VNC. Remote Desktop allows a user to view a remote computer screen and interact with it as if they were physically in front of it, when in reality they are only viewing a visual representation of the host computer. In other words, the only data that is passed between the host and client is graphical (with optional audible) data and key commands.

This "visual only" concept that the Remote Desktop brings to Windows XP adds an important part to the operating system. Previously, you would need third-party software or a high bandwidth connection to reliably, efficiently, and economically work from home or on the road. With the advent of Remote Desktop, you can quickly make a connection and perform administrative duties, even over a dial-up connection.

The Remote Desktop feature also incorporates the multiuser function that is new in Windows XP. Although only one person can be logged on at a time, including locally, the operating system keeps each user's applications running in the background when another user is logged in. In order to reaccess the application, a remote or local user simply has to log back into a disconnected session.

There are several advantages to this technology, which include the following:

* Employees can work directly on the workstations physically located at the office, but they can do so from home or on the road. In addition to the convenience, this eliminates the need to transfer huge files and also keeps proprietary or sensitive data at the workplace instead of on laptops and home PCs.

* If several employees require a program but use it only rarely, then Remote Desktop can eliminate the need for multiple licenses by providing a single, central server to which they can connect (make sure that this is supported in your software license agreement).

The Remote Desktop connection can be made in one of two ways. The first method works with a client program that is included on the Windows XP CD-ROM. This is the default method for setting up and creating a Remote Desktop session on a client computer. However, there are situations where a user is at a remote computer at which she cannot install programs or where the Windows XP Professional CD-ROM is unavailable. Fortunately, in this case a client can use Internet Explorer to connect to a Web Server with the Remote Desktop Web Connection software installed. The Remote Desktop Web Connection software turns the remote Web browser into a client program (i.e., a Web-based "front end"), thus greatly expanding the potential locations from which a user can connect. Because the security implications of the two methods are disparate, we will cover them in separate sections below.

Although Remote Desktop helps to make Windows XP a more comprehensive operating system, it also creates several security issues. In fact, the Remote Desktop can be considered a "backdoor." Popular backdoor hacking applications such as Trojan horses have many of the same functions as the Remote Desktop. This is why proper setup and configuration of Remote Desktop is essential. Issues such as account permissions, password strength, and even the creation of connection files can all result in a compromised system. Security guidelines will be covered at the end of this chapter.

Requirements

There are several requirements for a client to successfully connect to a Remote Desktop. Depending on how the connection is made (i.e., Web-based, front-end, or client application), those needs are different.

Host Requirements

The host requirements are:

- Windows XP Professional installed
- Proper permissions assigned to all users
- Access to the connecting computer via a Local Area Network (LAN), modem, or Virtual Private Network (VPN)

Client Requirements (Program)

The client requirements vary by operating system and are:

- Windows 95/98/Me/NT/2000/XP:
    - Windows XP Professional CD-ROM (Autorun)
- Windows 3.1
    - Windows XP Professional CD-ROM (Special client directory)
- Windows NT 3.51
    - Network connection to the client setup folder in Windows XP
- Windows CE
    - Access to *www.microsoft.com/mobile/downloads/ts.asp*

- All Windows OSs
  - Access to the remote computer running Windows XP via a LAN, modem, or VPN

Web Server Requirements (Web)

The Web Server requirements are:

- Internet Information Server 4+
- Active Server Pages enabled
- Active TCP/IP connection to client and host computers
- Proper permissions

Client Requirements (Web)

The Client requirements are:

- Internet Explorer 4+
- WINS Server service or other naming service
- Active TCP/IP connection with Web Server

Setting up and using a Remote Desktop Connection can be very involved. Depending on the connection type and user skill, as an administrator you will need to help your users configure the connection for security. The next segment will go into more detail about how to set up each of the parts of the Remote Desktop Connection.

Installation and Setup of the Default Remote Desktop Connection

Remote Desktop requires a minimum of two parts to work: the *client* and the *host*. Each part must be installed on the corresponding computer in order for the connection to be successful.

 Caution

Each part must be on a separate computer. This is because there can only be one login at a time per computer. Although you can make the connection, the session you used to create the connection will be dropped.

Host Install

By default, Windows XP Professional will have the Remote Desktop program installed. It only needs to be configured and enabled to become active.

Host Setup

Although the Remote Desktop is installed by default, it is not enabled or configured for a connection. In order to make a computer accessible, the local user must set up the accounts that will be given permissions. When doing this, ensure that you do not enable an administrator account or an account with administrator rights.

The following is a list of steps that explain how to set up a computer running Windows XP Professional as host to a Remote Desktop connection. Because of the two different ways that Windows XP allows users to access the operating system, we have used the XP default for our instructions, with the Classic view settings in parentheses.

- Go to **Start ➤ Control Panel** (**Start ➤ Settings ➤ Control Panel**).
- Choose **Performance and Maintenance ➤ System (System)** as shown in Figure 3.1.

Figure 3.1
System Properties window.

- Click on the **Remote** tab.
- Check **Allow users to connect remotely to this computer** in the **Remote Desktop** frame. See Figure 3.2.

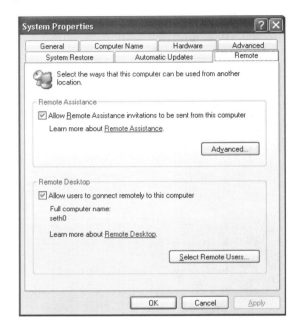

Figure 3.2
Remote Desktop frame.

- Click the **Select Remote Users** button. By default, the user account that is logged in will have access to the Remote Desktop. This allows you to leave your session running and to login remotely.
- Click the **Add** button (see Figure 3.3) to allow other users in your domain or home network access to your desktop session.

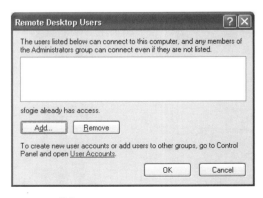

Figure 3.3
Remote Desktop Users selection screen.

- Object Types: Use this option to select other Users (e.g., your personal account) or Groups (e.g., Administrators) you wish to have access to your desktop session. See Figure 3.4.
- Locations: Use this option to search for and grant other Windows XP Professional computers on the network access to your desktop session.
- Object Names: User names, Account names, Domain\User names, Computer names, and more can be entered in this box. However, the names must be verified before they are accepted. This is done automatically, but you can check the names manually. If the name cannot be located on the computer or network, a **Name Not Found** dialog box will pop up. In this box you can update the information or remove the object from the list. See Figure 3.5.

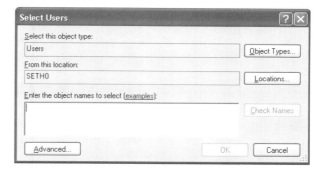

Figure 3.4
Select Users dialog window for Remote Desktop.

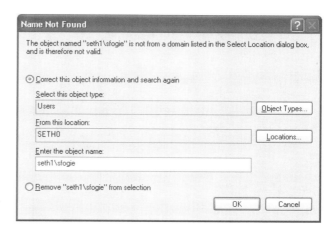

Figure 3.5
Name Not Found dialog window for Remote Desktop User selection.

- Advanced: This button lets you further your search for possible users to whom you want to give access. This would be used if you were not sure of the full object name (See Figure 3.6).

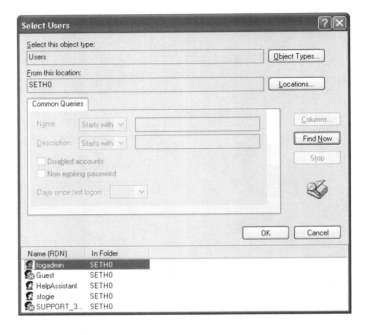

Figure 3.6
Select Users window (Advanced button).

- Once you have the desired users selected, click **OK** until you are out of the **System Properties** dialog box. Your desktop session is now set up for remote access.

Client Install

- Place the Windows XP Professional CD in the client's CD-ROM.
- If a Splash Screen appears when you put in the CD, skip to the next step. Otherwise, open **My Computer ➤ CD-ROM drive** and run **Setup.exe** by clicking on the icon shown in Figure 3.7.

Figure 3.7
SETUP.EXE icon

SETUP.EXE

- On the Windows XP Professional Splash Screen, shown in Figure 3.8, choose **Perform Additional Tasks**.

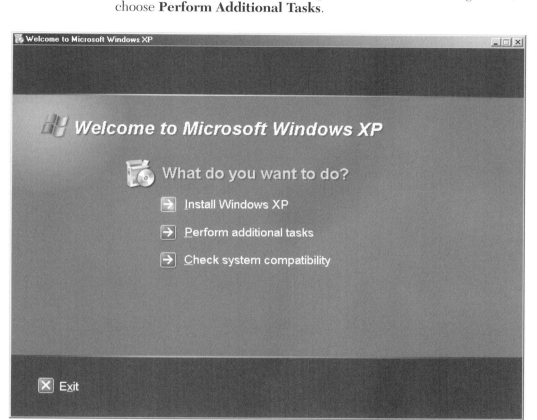

Figure 3.8
Windows XP Professional Splash Screen

- Click on **Set up Remote Desktop Connection** (Figure 3.9).
- Click **Next** and read the License Agreement. Once complete, click **Next** again.
- On the **Customer Information** screen, shown in Figure 3.10, you can set up Remote Desktop to be available either to you only or to anyone who uses your computer. This flexibility is useful in situations when non-trustworthy users will operate the computer. Make the appropriate selection and click **Next**.
- At this point the program is ready to be installed. If you are sure of the settings you selected, click the **Install** button to continue. See Figure 3.11.

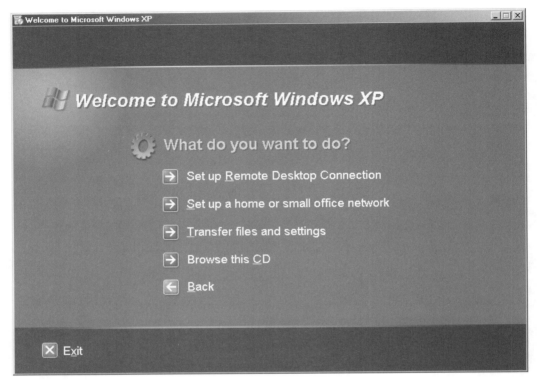

Figure 3.9
Windows XP Professional Splash Screen ("Perform additional tasks" button).

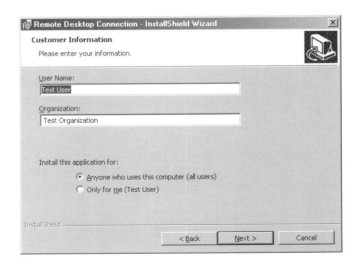

Figure 3.10
Remote Desktop Connection
window.

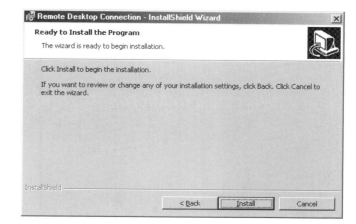

Figure 3.11
Remote Desktop Connection–
InstallShield Wizard.

- Upon completion of the install, you will be prompted to click a **Finish** button, and may be prompted to restart your computer, depending on the operating system version you are using.

Client Setup and Connection

- Once the Remote Desktop client application is installed, you can start it by going to **Start ➤ Programs ➤ Accessories ➤ Communication ➤ Remote Desktop**. This will open the Remote Desktop Connection window, shown in Figure 3.12.

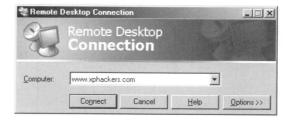

Figure 3.12
Remote Desktop Connection window.

- At this point you can either accept the default settings or adjust the connection options in the **Options** section of the **Remote Desktop** dialogue box. You can adjust the following settings:
  - General Settings—You can enter the user name, password, server, and domain of the computer to which you wish to connect, shown in Figure 3.13.

Figure 3.13
Remote Desktop Connection
(General Settings).

- Display—Depending on your own monitor settings and connection quality, you may want to turn down the screen size and color depth.
- Local Resources—This is where you disable/enable sounds, keyboard shortcuts, and peripheral connectivity. See Figure 3.14.

Figure 3.14
Remote Desktop Connection (Local
Resources).

- Programs—In certain situations you may wish a program to launch when you connect. For example, you may want Internet Explorer to always be ready for use when you make a connection. See Figure 3.15.

Figure 3.15
Remote Desktop Connection
(Programs).

- Experience—This tab allows you to set up the "extras" that come with a high-bandwidth connection. The better the connection, the more realistic your experience can be. See Figure 3.16.

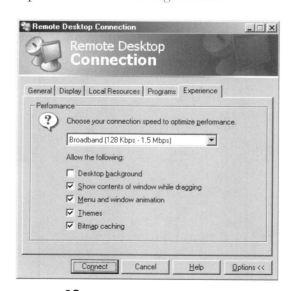

Figure 3.16
Remote Desktop Connection
(Experience).

Once you have all the settings the way you want them, hit the **Connect** button. This will open a window and bring you to a logon prompt (unless you specified this information in the General tab of the Options window).

Enter the User name and Password of the account you are using to create the session. See Figure 3.17.

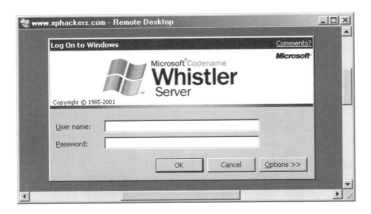

Figure 3.17
Log On to Windows.

 Caution

If there is someone else logged in, you will get a screen similar to Figure 13.8.

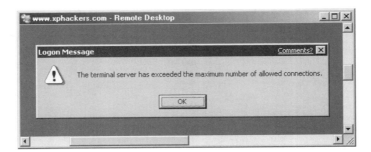

Figure 3.18
Logon Error Message.

At this point your connection should be established and you should be looking at the desktop of the remote computer. If you wish to view the session in a smaller window, you can do this by moving your mouse to the top of the remote desktop. This will drop a small bar down with the familiar minimize,

Figure 3.19
Pin icon.

down/up size, and close option. You will also see a pin, shown in Figure 3.19, that will "pin" the bar to the top of the screen permanently or allow the bar to hide when it is not needed.

Installation, Setup, and Creation of the Remote Desktop Web Connection

This feature allows a user to remotely access her desktop session from any computer that is connected to the host computer via a network connection. In the Remote Desktop Web Connection, the client only needs a browser (IE4+) and a TCP/IP connection to a Web Server with the Remote Desktop Web Connection software installed and running.

This connection, made with an ActiveX control, several ASP pages, and a few other files, offers users several advantages, which include the following:

- **Ease of deployment of client program**—Setting up and installing the client software can be as easy as sending someone an email or instant message with the proper URL. There is no need for a disk or prepackaged install program.

- **Global user freedom**—Since all that is needed is an Internet connection and a browser, a client can make a connection to a desktop from anywhere at anytime.

- **Economic application delivery**—Due to the ease of deployment, a Remote Desktop Web Connection can serve as the most economic and efficient means of application testing, development, and delivery to remote clients.

However, the Remote Desktop Web Connection has innate disadvantages as well. Due to the nature of the Web connection, there will be more processing time and slower delivery of graphical data. However, the Remote Desktop Web Connection may be the only solution for many users in mission-critical situations.

Installing the Web Components

Installation of the Remote Desktop Web Connection is threefold. The first part, the Windows XP host, is installed by default and only needs to be properly configured. This is covered in the Remote Desktop Connection Installation section. The second part is the client software that is downloaded as an ActiveX component when the connection is made, which will be covered later in this chapter. The third part, the Web interface, may require installation instructions. Due to different "Views" (i.e., New XP or Classic), we have included the Classic instructions in parentheses.

 Tip

> *IIS is installed on Windows XP Professional by default.*

 Tip

> *You must be logged in as an Administrator and have proper network policy settings in order to install this software. If you are restricted, contact your Network Administrator to continue.*

Installing the Remote Desktop Web Software

(Note: This procedure may require the Windows XP Professional CD)

- Click **Start ➤ Control Panel ➤ Add or Remove Programs** (**Start ➤ Settings ➤ Control Panel ➤ Add or Remove Programs**)
- Click **Add/Remove Windows Components**
- Select **Internet Information Services (IIS)**. See Figure 3.20.
- Click on the **Details** button and select **World Wide Web Services** from the list of subcomponents. See Figure 3.21.

 Caution

> *Only install the services that are needed. Adding extra services, like the Printers virtual directory, increases the chance of compromise.*

- Click again on the **Details** button and ensure that the **Remote Desktop Web Connection** is selected.

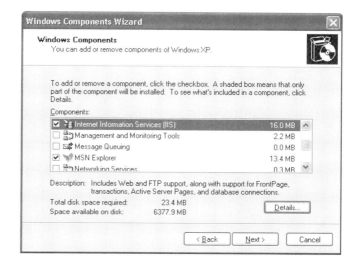

Figure 3.20
Installing IIS using the Windows Component Wizard.

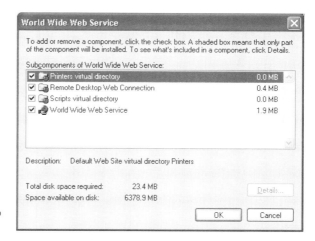

Figure 3.21
Subcomponents of World Wide Web component.

- Click **OK** (two times) and click the **Next** button.
- IIS will start installation, as shown in Figure 3.22.
- Once complete, click **Finish** and close the **Add or Remove Programs** window.
- Click **Start ➤ Control Panel ➤ Performance and Maintenance ➤ Administrative Tools ➤ Internet Information Services** (**Start ➤ Settings ➤ Control Panel ➤ Administrative Tools ➤ Internet Information Services**).

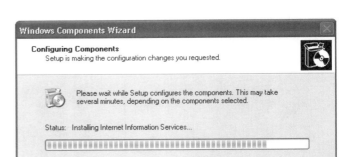

Figure 3.22
IIS Installing window.

* Expand the directories until you find the **tsWeb** folder (*local computer name*\Web Sites\Default Web Site\tsWeb). See Figure 3.23.

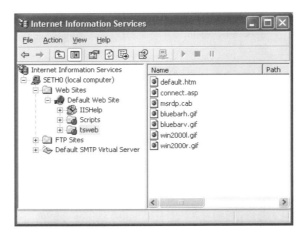

Figure 3.23
Internet Information Services Management console.

* Right-click on the **tsWeb** folder and select **Properties**.

* Click on the **Directory Security** tab, as shown in Figure 3.24.

* Click the **Edit...** button in the **Anonymous access and authentication control** section.

* Check the **Anonymous access** check box at the top of the dialog box, as shown in Figure 3.25.

Figure 3.24
IIS tsWeb folder properties.

Figure 3.25
Remote Desktop Authentication
Methods screen.

 Tip

> *Using Anonymous Access tells the IIS server to use the account designated as Anonymous. By using this account, any client is restricted to only those resources that the anonymous account is permitted to access, which is typically only Web pages or scripts needed by a Web page.*

- Click **OK** twice to exit.

Once IIS and tsWeb is installed and the permissions are set up, your Remote Desktop Web Connection is ready for operation.

Creating the Remote Desktop Web Connection

In order to successfully create a Remote Desktop Web Connection, you must have both a connection from the client computer to the Web Server where the tsWeb application is installed and a network connection from the Web Server to the host computer you wish to remotely control. Once these requirements are met, it is relatively simple to make the connection.

- Open Internet Explorer 4+.

- In the address bar, type **http://Web server address/tsWeb** and hit **Enter**. This should load a screen similar to Figure 3.26.

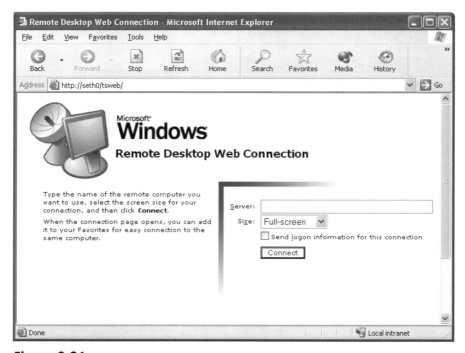

Figure 3.26
The Remote Desktop Web Connection Web page.

- On the Remote Desktop Web Connection screen you will need to provide the following information:
  - **Server:** This is the location or IP address of the computer to which you wish to connect.
  - **Size:** This is the initial screen size. The size may have to be adjusted depending on the resolution you have set on the client computer.
  - **Logon information:** This provides you with the option of entering a user name and domain name to use when making the connection, as shown in Figure 3.27.

Figure 3.27
Additional Logon options available for Web connection.

- Click the **Yes** button on the **Security Warning** dialog box (if it appears).

  Caution

If this is the first Remote Desktop Web Connection made with the client computer, an ActiveX Security dialog box will be presented similar to Figure 3.28. This warning is standard when an ActiveX program is run on any computer. If you wish to continue with the Web connection, you must accept the ActiveX component. (See security issues for more information on this.)

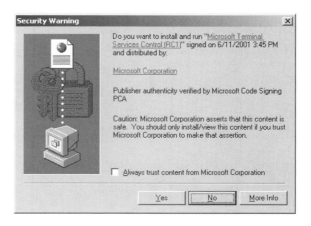

Figure 3.28
ActiveX Security Warning window.

- Select the option to connect your local drives and/or ports to the remote computer. See Figure 3.29.

51

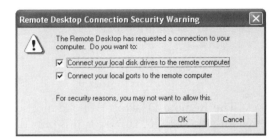

Figure 3.29
RDC Security Warning window.

 Caution

The option to connect your local drives and ports to the remote computer is available in case you want your resources to be available to the remote computer. This is beneficial if you want to have the ability to pass files from the remote computer to the local computer or vise versa. However, this opens security issues, such as the potential spread of computer viruses and worms (see the security issues section).

If the setup was successful, you will be presented with the familiar Log On to Windows dialog box. At this point the connection is ready to be made. If you have a problem establishing the connection, go to the troubleshooting section of this chapter.

If someone is logged in to the computer to which you wish to connect, you will be warned of the session's existence and that your new session will disconnect the current one at the local machine. Once you initialize the remote session (Figure 3.30), the local user will be presented with a window alerting them to your remote session.

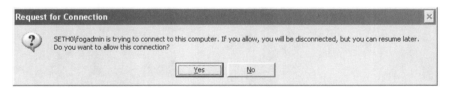

Figure 3.30
Request for Connection popup window that appears on host computer.

They will have a few seconds to deny your session before they are automatically logged out. In addition, the local user can log you out at any time by logging back into the computer. If this happens, you will be disconnected abruptly and a dialog box will be displayed alerting you to the reason of your disconnection, as shown in Figure 3.31.

Figure 3.31
Remote Desktop Disconnect popup
on local computer.

The Remote Desktop Web Connection is different in many ways from the client-side version. However, it is only different until the connection is made. Once the session is open, the overall concept is the same. Graphical data is sent to the client, and keyboard/mouse commands are sent to the host. This keeps both the data and the processing burden on the host computer, which serves to reduce the amount of information sent via the connection and maintains a higher level of security and integrity by keeping the data in one place.

In situations where a standard connection is not available, the Remote Desktop Web Connection is invaluable. However, with the increase in usability comes an equally important increase in security risks. As with all computers connected to the Internet, misconfiguration, simple passwords, or a complete lack of passwords will attract hackers and will invariably lead to compromise.

Breaking the Remote Desktop Connection

Regardless of the method used to connect to the Remote Desktop, the procedure for disconnection is the same. At the top of the window through which the Remote Desktop session is viewed, whether it be a browser or the default client program, there are the three familiar buttons that allow you to close, resize, and minimize the screen. They work the same for the Remote Desktop session as they do in any program, with the exception of the Close button. If you hit this button while the session is open, you will be disconnected from the remote session.

Note: The session will only be disconnected, not terminated. This small nuance can be confusing for users who take for granted that clicking an "X" will close and kill the target program. Windows XP has this feature to separate the act of killing the remote session from killing the logon session.

You can also terminate the session through the ironically named **Start** button. Instead of the Log Off and Turn Off option, you also have the ability to Disconnect, which kills the remote session, but leaves you logged in with all the programs running.

To permanently close the Remote Desktop Connection, you will have to Log Off the remote computer. This will terminate the remote session and the session on the host computer, which means that all open programs will also be closed.

Security Issues with the Remote Desktop Connection

There are several security issues that need to be addressed when deploying the Remote Desktop. Although Remote Desktop will help revolutionize the modern work paradigm, it will come at a potential cost to security. For example, misconfigured programs and poorly chosen passwords are the direct cause of over 90% of reported computer intrusions. The ease of the Remote Desktop Connection only magnifies this problem.

The subsequent pages will explain in detail the following security issues surrounding the Remote Desktop Connection.

- Improper account permissions
- Weak passwords
- Connecting local drives
- ActiveX components
- Saving connection files

Improper Account Permissions

The first thing you should ensure is that the account you are making the connection with is not an Administrator account. Although this account gives you full control over a computer, if a hacker cracked the password he would also have full access to your computer. In addition to the compromise of data, an account with full rights could be used by a hacker or malicious Web site to install a Trojan or virus on the client and host computer. The permissions associated with the logged-in user determine where and how a file is written to the hard drive. This effectively turns the Remote Desktop session into a hole through which a hacker could insert malicious code onto the host computer. For this reason you should not use an Administrator account or an account that was given administrator-level privileges.

Caution

Never use or give out an Administrator account when setting up a Remote Desktop Connection. This is rule number one when attempting to securely configure any operating system or program.

Weak Passwords

Another potential security weakness that cripples a Remote Desktop Connection is the use of weak passwords. Although your users can set up a Remote Desktop Account with a blank password, they will not be able to connect to the host with this account (Figure 3.32). Nevertheless, careless or improperly trained users can still set up an account with a weak password.

Figure 3.32
Account restriction warning as a result of blank password.

Of all the possible issues that network administrators have with the users for which they are responsible, weak passwords remain the biggest headache. Most commonly, people will choose the same password as their user name. These weak passwords can quickly be attacked and cracked by even the most untalented hacker. For this reason you should always use at least a six-character password with at least one uppercase letter, one lowercase letter, and one numerical character. While this will keep most hackers away, adding extra nonalphanumeric characters (e.g. !,@,#...) will make your password all the more secure. There are numerous tools on the Internet that can help you create strong passwords. Sites such as SecurityFocus.com and even Download.com have free programs that will create strong multicharacter passwords.

Connecting Local Drives and Peripherals to the Host Computer

When you make the Remote Desktop Connection, you will be asked if you want to "Connect your local disk drives..." and "...your local ports to the remote computer," shown in Figure 3.33. The benefits of this option are palpable. With your local file and peripheral resources available to the host com-

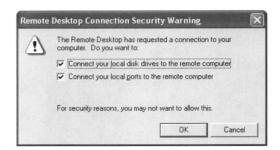

Figure 3.33
Remote Desktop Connection Security Warning.

puter, you can expand your foundation. Not only can you transfer and access files on both the local and host systems, but you can also use programs on the host system and save the files to your local system. In situations where several people share a graphic program, this could save time and money. In addition to the ability to share files, you can also print from the host computer to your local printer or upload files to your Palmtop or even send songs to your MP3 player.

However, by allowing this connection to exist, you may also be opening a Pandora's box. If it is so easy for you to connect and transfer files, it will be just as easy for a worm or Trojan to find its way to your local computer from the host computer. A simple execution of an infected file could inadvertently infect files across the remote desktop connection. Although this danger can be reduced with the use of virus protection and a cautious attitude when it comes to opening unknown files, the danger will still be a concern to you.

ActiveX Components

ActiveX allows a programmer to package, or compile, his code into components that can be simply integrated with other programs. In the case of the Remote Desktop Web Connection, the ActiveX component houses the pieces needed to connect the client computer to the host computer. Although the advantages of ActiveX components have proven themselves in many areas of programming, the Internet has introduced a negative aspect to the ActiveX component.

When you access a Web page with an integrated ActiveX component, you will be presented with a warning alerting you to the fact that you are about to download and run a program. This warning window also allows you to verify the owner of the ActiveX program (in case the ActiveX component is linked to the Web site from another location), and to learn more about the author of the program to ensure your safety. The option to refuse the ActiveX component is available by hitting the **No** button, and since all the information that you could

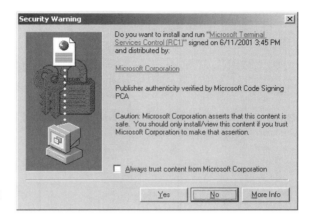

Figure 3.34
Microsoft's ActiveX Security Warning window.

hope to know about the purpose and author are readily available, one would assume that ActiveX components are fairly safe. This is true until you add in the human annoyance factor. Because Internet users see this type of warning fairly often, they are prone to simply accepting the warning and hitting **Yes** without really reading the details (see Figure 3.34).

In the case of the Remote Desktop Web Connection, the user must hit **Yes**. This is not dangerous by itself (with the exception of spoofed authentication); however, if you are not paying attention to the site you are visiting, this could lead to problems. If a hacker knows that a Web site is running a Remote Desktop Web Connection, it would be a fairly simple thing for them to purchase a domain with a misspelling of the valid domain and set up an ActiveX component of their own that could do anything to your computer. Although you may think this is far fetched, there are many sites that use this human error factor to get visitors. Sites like whitehouse.com (whitehouse.gov) and Webcrawer.com (Webcrawler.com) are some examples of misleading domains. For this reason, you must always be sure to read the fine print of any ActiveX component that you allow to run on your computer.

Saving Connection Information

When you use the Remote Desktop client program that comes on the Windows XP CD, you have the option to save your session connection information, as shown in Figure 3.35. While it is true that this could speed up your connection time, this is also a direct path for a hacker to access your remote computer. Given the ease at which a hacker or Trojan could gain unauthorized access to your computer, it would be a simple thing for someone to gain access

Figure 3.35
Remote Desktop Connection
(Connection settings).

to this file. For example, a malicious coder could design a Trojan that searches for the file named **default.rdp** in the **My Documents** folder and attaches it to an outgoing email. Similarly, a hacker can use Web page programming to illegally attach the file to form submission.

This problem arises when you save your password, user name, and other important information in the general settings of your Remote Desktop Web Connection options window. If this information is entered and you check the **Save my password** option, anyone can quickly access your remote desktop.

Even if you do not explicitly choose to save your settings, the session options are saved by default. Do not be fooled by this and never choose the option to save a password for anything in Windows.

To illustrate this, Figure 3.36 shows you the content of a saved Remote Desktop Connection file that includes the password. As you can see, it is an easy thing to glean the user name and location of the computer running the host side of the Remote Desktop software. Although the password may seem cryptic, most neighborhood Internet cracking sites will have programs to decrypt any password in a Remote Desktop file.

Document - WordPad

File Edit View Insert Format Help

Arial   8   Western   **B** *I* U

```
screen mode id:i:2
desktopwidth:i:1280
desktopheight:i:1024
session bpp:i:16
winposstr:s:0,1,0,0,1125,879
auto connect:i:0
full address:s:www.xphackers.com
compression:i:1
keyboardhook:i:2
audiomode:i:0
redirectdrives:i:1
redirectprinters:i:1
redirectcomports:i:0
redirectsmartcards:i:1
displayconnectionbar:i:1
username:s:peikari
domain:s:WWW
alternate shell:s:
shell working directory:s:
disable wallpaper:i:1
disable full window drag:i:1
disable menu anims:i:1
disable themes:i:0
bitmapcachepersistenable:i:1
password
51:b:01000000D08C9DDF0115D1118C7A00C04FC297EB010000007353A05E01952F4A8495F892CB7E4135000
0000008000000700073007700000003660000A80000001000000C00374AE82A649C9B93F8CD4532D103C00
00000004800000A000000010000000EC1C83F038C00717547BB3F7AA80512008020000261FADDBF89BD5D2
78B9C7DFF5483390E97B7F849B2883990597B63CDC0315BEAA215EB393DA4B4568C39C23171CC1E6BF8F35
C0A226C999183A6BFF18D8AFFEEF43EEB1F6D18B8541FE3257C535B24814B6B93C035BF936866A517A70ED
FCE2CD55901F1372379440160F61D0BA0503CEAE4F4572DE2FBE8808DFEEBA6998CD867DB1EFD719C64ECC
3614C7D299B0D95E48043E5D0154473C31CB0247075EB4DF6831858208C84F63D0BE597655D392F2F22AAC
E333379451C7DBE5D49FAE16BF1175F7313493940A15EA18742BECC6C519E65D11890947366B39BA20318B
BE2460449A7A603425DD4BF68347FF39A0A698D3957B3A8296A9B455646E84020228B013331AA61C5EAA5
6AFBD8D3B782B8BEC40979A7532AE83249C1DF2CC6C6FBF064C87430789A98B5D182B613F63BAEFD78290
EE3EB542AB03F1BB222AAC5AA7B595F3ED3DCF17C9183231024CC26A349463EF1978B77F955B91BE79950
A3C6CC4DACF351263475301090255292AA39C8FFAB4E76BF4C4A3B4A4E98401309DFE6249A4239FD8F757
FE3222584EEA9B4B39B6D845B61D5A2400D3EDBC132AD5004802AB7544DE461B709E735D68B26331 9F61F7
D0732E0C66FF51B514E1A7FD434D4E61A9D303EEC2094D89749C1A5B69F72E1E86AD7AA324A5E77B6D4CA
EE66217ED98BEC7BD752A11CD594E9C22587CBFEB0C126B700D0D01D4A2E9E5A84EED8861679486C7E3140
00000F741EF5C6454DF9511A0C5A5BE5B17A46EB47EBF
```

For Help, press F1   NUM

Figure 3.36
Remote Desktop Web connection.

Troubleshooting the Remote Desktop Connection

The Remote Desktop Connection by nature lends itself to numerous problems due to the fact that it relies heavily on existing networks. Because of this, you will inevitably have a problem at some point with your Remote Desktop Connection.

There are many different problems and error messages that you could come across using the Remote Desktop. Enough, in fact, that we could write a complete book on the subject. However, most of the errors will fall into one of five categories. The following will describe the most common errors and will point you in the right direction for a resolution.

- **Inadequate network connection:** As with all programs that rely on an existing network, the Remote Desktop will fall prey to bad network connections. The main categories of network problems are as follows:
  - Slow connection: This problem is one that everyone who has used the Internet has experienced. Usually, an overburdened network will cause a slow and choppy connection. In this case, the only options are to give up or "turn down" the quality on the connection via the client options.
  - No connection: If no connection is available at all, you may want to verify that the IP address settings are correct. In addition to this, if you are using a domain name, you must have access to a Domain Name Server to convert the domain name into its respective IP address.
  - Firewall present: If the client or host computers are behind a firewall, a connection may not be possible. This is because "compulsive" firewalls keep tight control over what data may pass back and forth from the network. The only solution in this case is to contact the person responsible for configuring the firewall and to politely request that your connection be allowed through.
- **Misconfigured settings:** This is a problem that you can fix. There are several key places that you will need to check to ensure that your connection settings are configured correctly.
  - Remote Desktop Client Program: If you have the wrong server name, user name, password, or an invalid startup program selected, you will not be able to make the connection.
  - Remote Desktop Host Program: In order for someone to make a connection to the host computer, they must have the Remote Desktop enabled and have an authorized account. To check these settings, right-click on the **My Computer** icon and select **Properties ➤ Remote** and configure the settings in the Remote Desktop frame.
- **Low resources:**
  - Inadequate hardware: As with all computer programs, a certain level of system resources must be available in order for proper execution to

be ensured. The limiting factors are usually RAM and processor speed. The requirements needed for the client program of the Remote Desktop software are listed in Table 3.1. In addition, the host computer must also meet a base level of RAM and processor speed to handle any incoming request.

Table 3.1. Hardware Requirements for the Client Program

OS	RAM	Processor
Windows 2000	32	Pentium
Windows NT 4.0	16	486
Windows 98	16	486
Windows 95	16	386
Windows for Workgroups 3.11	16	386

- Insufficient available memory: Windows uses what is known as virtual memory. This allows Windows programs to turn a part of the hard drive into a temporary storage space for data being used by programs. However, if there are too many programs running or RAM was not released back to the OS as programs are closed, your computer will eventually run out of RAM space or swap space. At the very least you will have to close as many open programs as you can; at most you will have to reboot to clear the problem.
- **Miscellaneous:**
  - Another user: If you are connected and your connection drops, you may be the victim of another user logging in locally. Local users have precedence.
  - Invalid licensing: If you are using Remote Desktop for more than one user, you will need proper licensing. This requires a licensed server, a connection to the server, and enough client licenses to support the number of users connecting to the host system.
  - No copy and paste: This problem is a known issue that a reinstall of the client will quickly fix.
  - Screen saver errors: If the host is set up to have a screen saver, the client will not see it. Instead, it will see a black screen.

Caution

Do not use a password-protected screen saver on a client while using the remote desktop. Using it may lock you out of the computer.

Summary

Although Remote Desktop existed before Windows XP as the embryonic "Terminal Services," it has since grown significantly. This is good news for computer users that understand the security ramifications that improper use of the Remote Desktop can have. However, the ease at which a computer can become a host using the Remote Desktop will provide hackers with a fair share of targets from overzealous and undereducated users. If you are responsible for a network, be sure that your users understand how easily the Remote Desktop can be abused. Keeping a close eye on permissions, accounts, and saved Remote Desktop files can go a long way toward keeping your data secure.

Chapter 4

SECURING REMOTE ASSISTANCE

This chapter covers

- What is Remote Assistance?
- Requirements for Remote Assistance
- Sending a Remote Assistance call
- Accepting a Remote Assistance call
- Security issues surrounding Remote Assistance
- Common errors that may occur when using Remote Assistance

Overview

As a network administrator, technical support can take up a lot of your time. Until now, supporting remote users usually meant purchasing multiple copies of Symantec's expensive *PC-Anywhere* software. Microsoft has changed all this with its new *Remote Assistance* feature in its .NET Server client, Windows XP. Remote Assistance allows support technicians to provide visual, remote technical support. By adding features that you have always wanted and expected in an operating system, Microsoft has tried to create the total operating system "experience," as they like to call it.

The addition of Windows XP Remote Assistance revolutionizes the technical support field. With a few simple commands, the technician has full access to the user's computer. However, remote access does have the potential for frightful security breaches. Though designed as an administration tool, the Remote Assistance program acts like Trojan horses used by hackers to gain unauthorized access to a computer. All it takes is one misconfigured invitation to fall into the wrong hands and the hacker owns the originating computer.

Not to be confused with Remote Desktop, which only allows one active session at a time per client (or per license on .NET Server), Remote Assistance will allow both the owner and the remote user to control the computer at the same time. Options such as chatting via keyboard or microphone show that Remote Assistance was designed more for technical support than for remote administration. The ability for the local user and remote user to communicate while viewing the same desktop makes technical support easy, and even pleasurable—if you are like the majority of network administrators who enjoy taking the time to help their users.

During the remainder of this chapter, the requesting party will be the "Novice" and the assisting party will be the "Helper." We adopt the terms used by Microsoft in the Remote Assistance program.

Requirements for Remote Assistance

There are several requirements that are needed by both the Helper and the Novice in order for Remote Assistance to work. These requirements include the following:

- The Helper and the Novice computers must both be running Windows XP.
- In order to receive an acceptance notice of the invitation, the Helper must be connected to the Internet.
- Depending on the Invitation delivery method, the Novice will need either Windows Messenger, a MAPI email program, or a means of delivery for a file.
- If the Helper or Novice is behind a firewall, the firewall will need to be configured to allow Remote Assistance traffic via outbound TCP port 3398.
- Proper configuration of Remote Desktop properties must be set if remote control is required.
- A strong password is needed by the Helper to establish the initial connection to the Novice.

Although the requirements are few, a connection can be difficult to create if either the Helper or Novice is part of a corporate network. End-users behind a corporate firewall may require help in setting up remote assistance. This is due to the level of security needed to ensure data integrity in the enterprise. If Remote Assistance is necessary and your users cannot establish a connection due to current firewall settings, you will need to make sure that the firewall allows port (3398 Outbound TCP) from the client in order to successfully establish a connection.

Using Remote Assistance

Once you meet all the requirements for Remote Assistance, it is time to make the connection. Because security is such an important issue when dealing with the remote control of a computer, the Remote Assistance program necessitates more than just a simple point-and-click approach to establishing the connection. There are several checkpoints along the way that give the Novice (owner) the option of preventing the connection from being made.

Sending the Invitation

The first step in setting up a Remote Assistance session is to send a call for help.

- Click on **Start ➤ Help and Support**, which will open a window similar to Figure 4.1.

 Tip

The Help and Support Center is new to Windows XP. It is designed to help the user easily and quickly access the many different aspects of Help available in the Windows OS.

- Click on the link **Invite a friend to connect to your computer with Remote Assistance**.
- Select the type of Invitation you wish to use to send to the technician (see Figure 4.2):

65

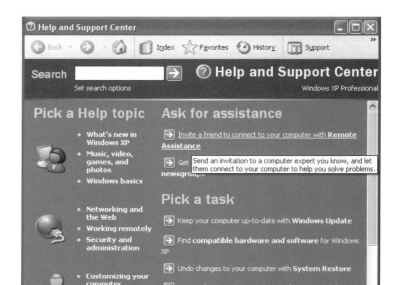

Figure 4.1
Windows XP Help and
Support Center.

Figure 4.2
The Remote Assistance
Invitation methods.

- **Windows Messenger**: To use this option the Helper and Novice must have MSN Messenger installed and have an active and open connection between the two messengers.
- **Email**: To use this option, the Novice and Helper must have a MAPI-based email program on their computers (e.g., Outlook Express, Outlook).
- **File**: To use this option, the Novice and Helper must have a means of delivery for the invitation file that will be created.

File Invitation

- Enter a name.

 Tip

You should never use your real name when sending an Invitation. A pseudonym adds an extra layer of protection in case your Invitation is hijacked. Providing your real identity (as shown in Figure 4.3) will only help a hacker find your computer more quickly.

- Choose the time limitation.

 Tip

For security reasons, it is important to choose a limited time length availability as shown in Figure 4.3. The shortest you can tolerate (while balancing convenience) is the best.

Enter a strong password (i.e., any word that is not found in a dictionary, is greater than 6 characters, and includes uppercase, lowercase, numerical, and one of the following: !@#$%^&°()), which will be required when the Remote Assistance connection is made. You will need to provide the password to the Helper via another means of communication.

 Caution

Although you can disable the password option, it is not recommended. This is in case the Invitation ends up in the wrong person's hands. Without a strong password, the Novice computer could be easily breached (See Figure 4.4).

- Click **Save Invitation** to store the Invitation file on your hard drive or network.

Figure 4.3
Identity and Expiration
options for Invitation.

Figure 4.4
Remote Assistance password
options window.

Email Invitation

- Enter a name and message to be included in the Invitation email, as shown in Figure 4.5.

- You will be asked by Microsoft Outlook to allow the Remote Assistance program to check if the entered email address is in your address book. Click **Yes** to pass this.

 Tip

Because of the increase in popularity of Microsoft Outlook address book as a vector for computer viruses, Windows XP will verify that the Remote Assistance program is permitted to access the address book (Figures 4.6. and 4.7).

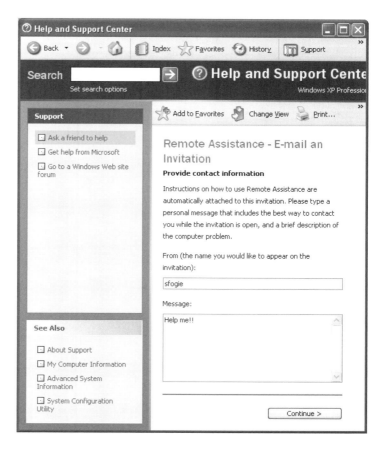

Figure 4.5
Remote Invitation email
message.

Figure 4.6
Microsoft Outlook Express's warning message.

Figure 4.7
Microsoft Outlook alert dialog box.

- Click **Send Invitation**.

Chat Invitation

- Open the Microsoft Messenger chat program.
- Click **Tools ➤ Ask for Remote Assistance** and click on the user to which you want to send the Invitation, as shown in Figure 4.8.

Figure 4.8
Sending Invitation via MSN Messenger Service.

Figure 4.9
Entering messenger address for
Invitation.

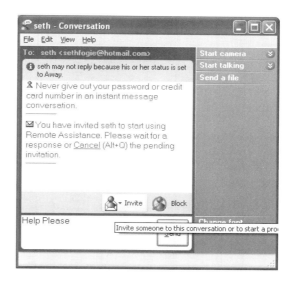

Figure 4.10
Sending the Remote Invitation
via chat.

- If the user is not listed, select **Other...** and enter the email address of the helper, as shown in Figure 4.9.

- Enter a message and click the **Invite** button. See Figure 4.10.

Tracking Invitations

When you send an invitation from the Help and Support Center, it is logged and stored on your computer. This is to provide a means for Windows XP to verify that any incoming Remote Assistance connection request is valid. Windows XP also keeps tabs on any unanswered Invitations in order to allow you the ability to Expire, Resend, Delete, or learn more about the Details of the Invitation.

To access this list, you need to perform the following steps:

- Click **Start ➤ Help and Support ➤ Invite a friend to connect to your computer with Remote Assistance ➤ View Invitation Status**. See Figure 4.11.
- Select one of the Invitation Options:
  - **Details**: This option provides you with all the information about the Invitation. It tells you how the Invitation was sent and to whom it was sent if applicable. It also provides you with the expiration time, open status, password status, and message included (see Figure 4.12).
  - **Expire**: This will simply change the status of the Invitation to "Expired."
  - **Resend**: In case the recipient never received the Invitation, or it was sent to the wrong location, this option allows you an easy way to recreate the Invitation.
  - **Delete**: As you can guess, this allows you to delete the Invitation. You may get a warning if the Invitation is still in "Open" status.

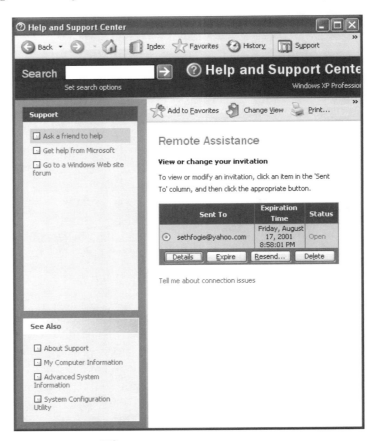

Figure 4.11
Viewing Remote Assistance invitation statuses.

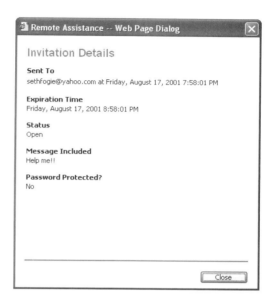

Figure 4.12
Remote Assistance Invitation Details.

Accepting the Remote Assistance Call

The first stage of security in Remote Assistance is the acceptance stage of the request for help. The request can only come via a file or email message.

There are three main ways to receive an invitation. Each of these will be covered in the following pages.

- **Chat:** When an invitation is sent via a Windows Messaging program, the requested party must be online. In addition, the party must accept the Invitation. Figure 4.13 illustrates the message that arrives bearing the invitation as a link. To accept, click the highlighted Accept link. This will send a message back to the initiating computer to start the Remote Assistance program.

- **Email:** When you receive an email message containing a Remote Assistance request, the actual request is included as an attachment. The attached file is the same file that would have been created if the requesting party chose to manually create a file and send it to the remote party. However, there is a message that is included by default with the email message that outlines some of the issues surrounding Remote Assistance. Included in the default message is a personal message from the sender. Figure 4.14 provides an example of a real request for Remote Assistance sent via email.

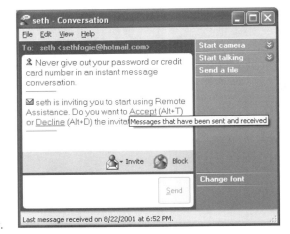

Figure 4.13
Receiving Remote Assistance request.

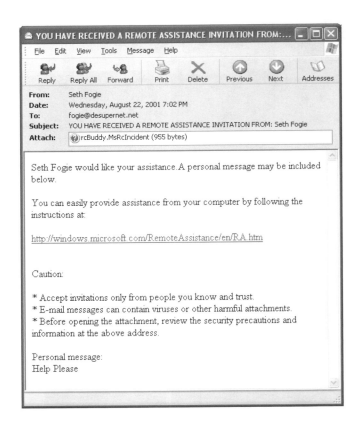

Figure 4.14
Request for Remote Assistance sent
via email.

Caution

As the initial instant message dialog warns, you should never give out password or credit card information via a chat program. This is because you never know who is on the other end, and your information could be easily "sniffed," or captured, as it passes on the Internet.

- Open the e-mail.

 Caution

The email Remote Assistance comes as an attachment that must be downloaded to the computer and executed. Unless you are sure the request is legitimate and are expecting it, you should be wary about using it. It could be a virus or Trojan in disguise. See Figure 4.15.

- Upon execution of the Remote Assistance invitation, a dialog with the sender's information will be displayed. If there is no password option, the sender did not require a password in the request for help. Otherwise, enter the password and click **Yes**. See Figure 4.16. This will start the initiation of the connection. This is the second stage of security that is built into Remote Assistance.

 Caution

The second line of security defense that Remote Assistance uses is authorization. The file and email methods both can require a password to make the connection. The chat method indirectly requires authentication because the request is made from a Windows Messenger account that itself requires authentication.

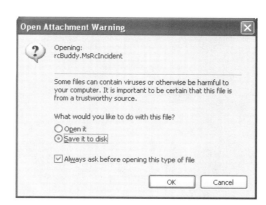

Figure 4.15
Open Attachment Warning for
Remote Assistance file.

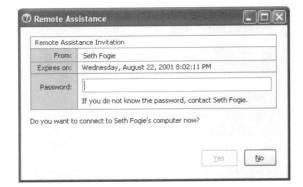

Figure 4.16
Remote Assistance Helper side connection verification.

Figure 4.17
Remote Assistance Helper connecting screen.

- **File:** Accepting the file method only requires that the remote party receive the Remote Assistance file and that they double-click it. This will open the same window as in Figure 4.17.

Using the Remote Assistance Connection

At this point in the connection process, two security checkpoints have been crossed. First, the explicit setup and delivery of the request acts as a security filter to limit the session time and permissions on the requesting computer. Second, the password option adds further security.

The next security checkpoint is the required active approval of the Remote Assistance connection by the Novice. Finally, the most critical security checkpoint is that needed to gain full control of the Novice's computer. This checkpoint is similar to the third in that it also requires an active acceptance of a request from the helper before control of the computer is passed to the helper.

To Start the Remote Assistance Session

1. **Helper**: Start the session by clicking on the file or the link sent by the Novice. See Figure 4.18.

2. **Novice**: Accept the Remote Assistance connection. See Figure 4.19.

3. Session is initiated and Remote Assistance screen is loaded on helper's computer; connection is established. See Figure 4.20.

4. **Helper and Novice**: Communicate via chat program that is built into Remote Assistance program. See Figures 4.21 and 4.22.

5. **Helper**: If the problem cannot be solved without remote control, the helper can initiate a command to give the helper remote control of the Novice computer.

6. **Novice**: Accepts or declines the request for Remote Control. See Figure 4.23.

Figure 4.18
Accepted Chat invitation on Novice computer.

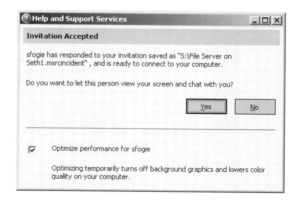

Figure 4.19
Accepted Remote Assistance file invitation on Novice computer.

 Caution

    Users should be educated to exercise extreme caution before giving someone else remote control over their computer.

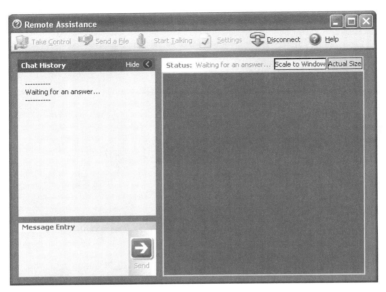

Figure 4.20
The Remote Assistance Window while waiting for authorization from Novice.

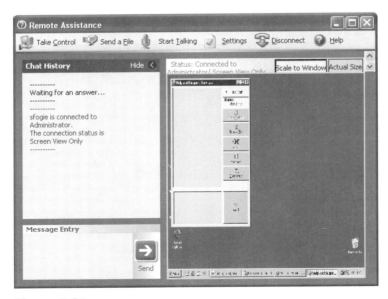

Figure 4.21
Remote Assistance screen on Helper's computer during session.

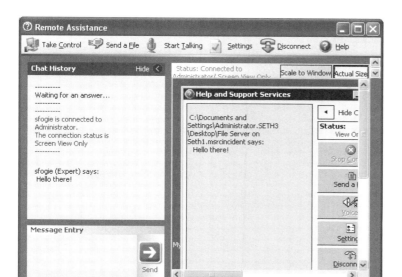

Figure 4.22
Remote Assistance chat session (left is Helper screen/right is Novice screen).

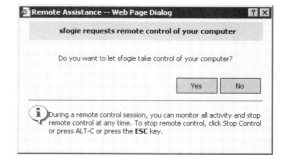

Figure 4.23
Remote Assistance remote control
warning.

7. **Helper**: Close the Remote Assistance—Web Page Dialog window (Figure 4.24) and proceed.

8. **Helper or Novice**: When the Novice's problem has been solved, click the Disconnect button to end the session. See Figure 4.25.

As you can see, the Remote Assistance program is fairly straightforward. The security considerations are well thought out and with the proper configuration will help maintain a secure connection.

The next segment offers pointers that will keep your Remote Assistance sessions secure.

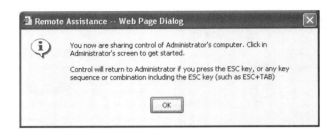

Figure 4.24
Remote Assistance dialog popup informing helper of acceptance of control request.

Figure 4.25
Remote Assistance control ended alert.

Remote Assistance and Security Issues

Allowing access to files and folders on a computer is a key part of any network. To do this securely, file servers are often set up using the NTFS file system; this enables an administrator to control who is and who is not allowed access to data on the server. The policy can be as liberal as allowing a user full control of all files or as limiting as allowing a user only read access to one file on the server.

Windows XP utilizes NTFS and file encryption. However, all it takes is one user account with elevated privileges in combination with Remote Assistance and all the effort spent in securing files is wasted. With Remote Assistance, a Helper has full control of all the files that the Novice has access to. While it is true that a Helper has to pass four different security checkpoints before they can get remote control of the computer, once in, it only takes a few seconds of unmonitored control and a Helper can make disastrous changes to the computer such as installing a permanent backdoor.

The following is a list of warnings to give to your users that employ the Remote Assistance feature of Windows XP:

*   **Never open a Remote Assistance request file without being 100% positive of its origin.** It is a simple thing for a hacker to create a fake

program that uses the Remote Assistance icon. If a message with the Remote Assistance icon shows up in your mailbox with a message from someone you know, it may be very tempting to double-click it to receive. Do not do this wantonly, as it could be a Trojan or virus that uses the same Remote Assistance icon.

- **Never send a Remote Assistance Invitation without a password.** This is like sending someone a postcard in the mail with an announcement of your intended vacation and then leaving your house unlocked. If the message, or file, ended up in the wrong hands, a malicious person could hijack the invitation and attempt to abuse the Helper status.

- **Be sure to use a strong password**. The Internet is full of hacker programs that can be used to guess your password. To prevent a successful guess, you must create a password greater than six letters, using at least one capital letter and one number (not in the first or last letter) with an optional nonalphanumeric character (e.g., hApp1ne&&, iLov3y°u). Increasing the length and varying the characters will significantly decrease the chance that your password is guessed.

- **Reduce the Remote Assistance Invitation time limit to as short as possible.** By reducing the time window, you are also reducing the chance that your invitation is abused. The less time a hacker has to exploit the connection, the less chance you have of being hacked.

- **Be completely sure to whom you are giving control.** Script kiddies (prehackers) gain bragging rights by "owning" more computers than their friends. This makes it worth their while to attempt to socially engineer a session from you.

- **Never enable Remote Assistance on a security-sensitive computer.** Any computer that contains mission-critical data should not be permitted to accept remote assistance calls. This facilitates the potential for a security breach. If assistance is necessary, an onsite support specialist with the proper clearance should be employed.

By keeping these few points in mind, you can increase the security of your Remote Desktop sessions. However, there are plenty of other problems that can arise from poorly configured settings or network connection issues. The next segment will cover several of the most common errors that a user could see and will suggest ways to fix the problems.

Troubleshooting Remote Assistance

Remote assistance can be problematic for numerous reasons. The following will break down the most common problems into categories and will provide a starting place when looking for solutions. Users should be educated on these issues.

Network Issues

- **No connectivity:** If a connection cannot be made between the Novice and Helper, there are several components to look at.
  - Firewall—If there is a firewall, the Remote Assistance connection may not be possible due to the current security policy (Figure 4.26). Check with your friendly Network Administrator to see if it is within the security policy to allow a Remote Assistance connection.

Figure 4.26
Remote Assistance (No connectivity).

  - Network Down—As with all networks, it is possible that yours is down. You can test this by trying to make a connection via the Windows Messaging service.
- **Slow connectivity**: If the connection between the Novice and Helper is lagging, there is not much that can be done. Fundamentally, it will be due to inadequate bandwidth. Whether as a result of an overloaded network or a low-bandwidth connection, there is not much that can be done other than to demote the audio settings if they are enabled (see Figure 4.27). This setting is adjusted using the Settings button on the Remote Assistance window on either the Novice or Helper side. In addition, you can ensure that all other Internet-based programs are closed or disabled.

Figure 4.27
Adjusting the Audio quality of the
Remote Assistance connection.

Misconfiguration Issues

- **Remote Control Fails**—If you cannot establish a Remote Control session but you know that you are connected, you will need to ensure that the Remote Desktop settings are correct by right-clicking on **My Computer** ➤ **Properties** ➤ **Remote** ➤ **Remote Desktop** and ensure that the **Allow users to connect remotely to this computer** option is checked. See Figure 4.28.

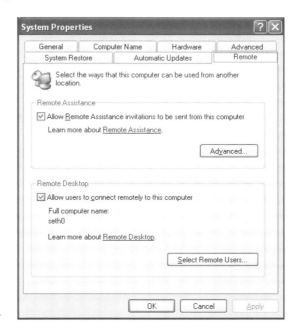

Figure 4.28
Remote Desktop properties windows.

- **Miscellaneous Errors**—If the settings for Remote Desktop are correct, other possible causes for a rejected connection are as follows:
  - The clock settings do not match or the time limit has expired (see Figure 4.29). Try to resend the Invitation and verify that the computer clocks match and that the date is correct.

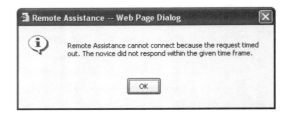

Figure 4.29
Remote Assistance (clock settings).

- Account not permitted to connect—Verify that the account has connect privileges under the Remote Desktop settings previously mentioned. See Figure 4.30.

Figure 4.30
Remote Assistance (account not permitted).

- File Error—If the file is already open or is corrupt, the Novice will have to resend the invitation. See Figure 4.31.

Figure 4.31
Remote Assistance (file error).

Summary

The new Windows XP Remote Assistance feature has the potential to revolutionize the technical support industry. The program is intuitive and powerful. However, with this increase in power there is a corresponding need for an increase in security. By educating users to configure the Novice computer to accept only those requests that are permitted and to maintain control over Remote Control permissions, you can help users maintain data integrity. The trickiest part of Remote Assistance for end-users will be to avoid spoofing or social engineering attempts. A hacker could easily trick a Novice user into allowing a connection and could thus gain unauthorized access to a network. If you or your employees have previously fallen for cleverly worded emails carrying viruses, you may become prey for devious hackers sending false invitations. Educate yourself and your employees not to accept unsolicited invitations.

Windows .NET Client Security: Protecting Windows XP

Spotlight: The "Raw Sockets" Controversy

Introduction

Recently, there has been an "urban myth" circulating that Windows XP will result in a digital Armageddon. This misunderstanding is based on the fact that Windows XP Home Edition ships with a powerful functionality called "raw sockets." This section explains the security implications of raw sockets and will attempt to separate fact from fiction.

What Are Raw Sockets?

"Raw Sockets" refers to the ability of the operating system (OS) to write raw IP packets used in network communication. This type of power gives the operator the ability to send data across a network with a fake return address on it. Commonly known as *spoofing*, this type of assault is used in distributed Denial of Service (DoS) attacks in which millions of mislabeled packets are hurled at a target network in order to render it inaccessible by legitimate traffic.

Typically, a user or program interfaces with a library file that controls the labeling of the packet. This prevents the packet from being corrupted and ensures that data transmission works. This also ensures that average users do not alter their data packets and disrupt the flow of data. An OS that supports raw sockets would allow you to rewrite any field in an IP packet.

What Does Windows XP Have to Do with Raw Sockets?

Windows XP is the first Windows home operating system to ship with default Raw Socket functionality built in. Opponents of raw sockets claim that the widespread availability of Windows XP Home Edition computers will provide fertile grounds for hackers to sow their DoS tools. These opponents argue that the average Windows home user is neither intelligent nor skilled enough to protect their personal computers from hackers. Thus, argue the raw socket opponents, with the release of Windows XP, Microsoft will unleash a potential army of zombie machines upon the world.

Before the .NET era, the average home user ran Windows 3.1/95/98/Me. On the other hand, the power user ran Windows NT/2K. This disparity created a gulf that caused many problems for software vendors. Microsoft had for years been searching for a common code base to use for both the home and office versions of Windows. With the release of Windows XP, Microsoft's vision for a unified operating system came true.

In addition to attempting to bring together the two very different markets into one version of Windows, Microsoft has also been trying to incorporate as many features as possible into their operating system. It is a fact that UNIX-based operating systems have had raw sockets capability for years. In fact, Windows 2000, not Windows XP, was the first Microsoft operating system to allow native raw socket support.

The problem with raw sockets arises with the one simple requirement to gain access to the raw IP packets, namely, Administrator privileges on the target computer. With Windows 2000, UNIX, and even Windows XP Pro, the Administrator account should only be used in situations where you have complete control. Ideally, users should delegate routine tasks to less powerful accounts. This prevents any user or program from accidentally deleting or altering important files.

However, the Windows XP Home version is run under the Administrator account by default. This means that any user or program on a computer using the Home version is able to create raw sockets. This offers hackers a great number of computers to attack and use in distributed denial of service assaults. Using these high-bandwidth home computers, one master Trojan or virus could easily create spoofed packets to flood a hapless target.

Is the Threat Real?

Most security experts agree that there is no significantly increased threat from native raw socket support in Windows XP Home Edition. The fact that the feature has been present in computers for decades, in conjunction with the added security features in Windows XP, makes it improbable that hackers will target raw sockets much more than before. In fact, over the last few years other methods of attack have made a much larger impact on the global computing community. Code Red, ILoveYou, Melissa, and other malicious programs have already caused billions of dollars of damage.

In addition, a skilled attacker can gain root (Administrative) access to greater than 95% of the world's networked machines. Once an attacker has control of a machine, she can install any available functionality. Thus, the raw socket functionality has been readily available in previous versions of Windows for years.

Summary

The security risk of native raw socket support in Windows XP Home Edition is minimal. This functionality has been available for years, and to date there is no evidence to suggest a causal link between Windows XP and an increase in DoS attacks. Network administrators should be aware of the existence of raw sockets in Windows XP, but they should not fear it.

Frequently Asked Questions

Q: I am the administrator of a large NT network. Our company CIO has stated that we cannot upgrade to Windows .NET Server because of "significant security concerns" from raw sockets. He is convinced that installing Windows XP Pro on existing and new workstations would be an increased security risk, since we are on a network behind a corporate proxy and firewall setup.

A: Your CIO's fears are unfounded for several reasons. To begin with, the raw sockets controversy centers on home editions of Windows XP, not Windows XP Professional or .NET Server deployed in an enterprise. In addition, since you are behind a firewall and proxy, you have additional layers of protection. Finally, older implementations of Windows (such as NT) are inherently insecure, and upgrading to Windows XP will dramatically enhance the overall level of security for your network.

Q: Many of our employees use Windows XP Home Edition at home. What advice can I give them about raw sockets?

A: The best protection for users is careful education. You can remind your users of the following best safety practices:

1. It is good security practice to avoid using the Administrator account for anything. It is better to use more restricted accounts unless absolutely critical.

2. As always, do not install or execute binaries unless you are sure they are not a virus or Trojan. A binary is an executable program. It usually has a .exe or .com extension, but when in doubt, ask for help.

3. Learn to use Windows XP's built-in firewall (ICF). Even if you do accidentally install a Trojan, when ICF is properly configured the Trojan cannot spoof your IP address.

4. Keep your virus and Trojan scanners up to date—and use them.

5. Read and stay educated on security matters. Education is always the best defense. Your brain is still the best security tool.

Chapter 5

THE INTERNET CONNECTION FIREWALL

This chapter covers:

- Overview of Microsoft's Internet Connection Firewall (ICF)
- Firewall review
- Enabling and disabling the ICF
- Adjusting Security, Program, ICMP, and Logging options
- Understanding the Log file
- Internet Connection Sharing and bridge connection issues for the ICF

Overview

A *personal firewall* can be defined as *a software micro-firewall that works at any level of the TCP/IP stack to selectively block all or part of either inward- or outward-bound traffic.* Although they have never been proven to provide a security benefit, personal firewalls are nevertheless a growing fad among home and small-business users. While ineffective from a security standpoint, the growing use of personal firewalls does have an important side effect: they raise the awareness of security issues for the average end-user.

Microsoft, eager to demonstrate its new commitment to security, has integrated its own easy-to-configure personal firewall directly into Windows XP. According to Microsoft, the target audience for their Internet Connection Firewall is the new user who has an always-on broadband Internet connection and who is not aware of security issues. The firewall has been designed to be as easy as possible to use in order to target nonsophisticated users. Microsoft has focused on streamlining the configuration process and on programming the majority of settings with common defaults.

However, as a network administrator, you should be aware of conflicts that the ICF can have for your users. Having a firewall built into the operating system is a potential source of conflicts both with your enterprise security measures and with third-party vendor firewall products. For example, a user might complain that he cannot receive Remote Assistance help, when in fact it is his own ICF that is blocking him.

Nevertheless, the ICF can be useful in managing specific security issues. For power users, the firewall offers enough protection to use as a key component of a home office or small business security plan. Because of its integration with Internet Connection Sharing (ICS) and the Bridge Connection, the ICF can ensure that its host computer (and network) remains separated from outside attacks.

 Caution

A Trojan horse on the protected side of the network can circumvent the ICF. The firewall will not protect against infected emails or vulnerabilities that are a result of third-party programs (e.g., Web Server software, FTP software, peer-to-peer sharing programs, etc.). In addition, the ICF will only block incoming requests for information, but will not block outgoing communication.

Firewall Review

Firewalls come in one of two basic forms: hardware and software. The average home or small-business user often utilizes the software version because it is less expensive and is easier to set up and install. Regardless of the type of firewall, they are analogous in that both types inspect data transfer through a network. However, that is where the similarities end.

There are two main methods of inspection, which are *stateful* and *static*. The differences between the two are found in what is known as the OSI Reference Model (Figure 5.1). Every packet entering a network comes in via wires or some other form of hardware. This is the Physical layer. The data

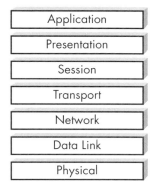

Figure 5.1
The OSI Reference Model.

then enters the Data Link layer, and continues on up the model until it reaches its destination at the Application layer. Each layer is responsible for certain parts of the delivery of information. The higher up the model, the closer the computer is to the actual data carried in the packet.

This model is important when examining firewalls because every firewall will use this model to perform its filtering. The following segments will describe briefly the key components of the static and the stateful firewall as well as the advantages and/or the disadvantages of each.

Static Firewall

The static firewall works by examining each packet at the Network layer (Figure 5.1) as it attempts to access a computer. By looking at the source and destination IP address and comparing them to a predefined list, the firewall will either permit or reject a packet. Although this method is effective for most purposes, it can be tedious to configure. Additionally, a static firewall can be tricked through IP spoofing. If a hacker fakes his IP address, or creates his own packets with one of the many hacker tools available on the Internet, the static firewall will think the packet is legitimate and will allow its passage.

Stateful Firewall

A stateful firewall also examines a packet at the Network layer and compares the source and destination IP address using a set of guidelines created by a network administrator. However, it goes one step further in that it also looks at the data the packet is carrying and protects the network up to the Application layer (Figure 5.1). This allows an internal computer to host a Web Service such as an email or FTP server. By ensuring that the data in the packet is valid, the firewall can prevent hackers from using the services as relay points to pass unauthorized data.

Also, as a stateful firewall processes incoming and outgoing packets, it records the origin of the connection. The connection tag is then compared against any other incoming packets that are destined for an internal computer to ensure that it is expected. This provides an extra layer of protection in case a hacker spoofs a packet or hijacks a connection.

In addition, a stateful firewall keeps all ports closed until an internal computer requires them. This type of protection effectively turns a computer invisible to those on the Internet ("stealth mode"). Unless a hacker happens to do a port scan when a connection is in use, the scan will come back blank.

The Internet Connection Firewall

The ICF is a stateful firewall. It keeps track of all connection requests from the Internet. If a computer from inside the network did not recently request data from an external computer attempting to make a connection, the external request will be denied.

If an external computer is making a request to an internal computer running a Web Server or FTP server, the firewall will ensure that a "service definition" exists for the request. The service definition includes information such as port, protocol, and IP address of the resources used by the internal computer (e.g., port 80, TCP for a Web Server). The ICF has many of the typical service definitions set up by default (e.g., Web Server, FTP Server, etc.). In addition, it allows for other custom service definitions.

The ICF keeps its host computer in stealth mode. By keeping all ports closed until the internal computer needs them, a hacker using a port scanner will think the IP address of the host computer is not in use.

Enabling and Disabling the ICF

The following will illustrate the steps required to enable and disable the ICF using its default settings. Following this segment, we describe in detail the different options available when using the ICF.

 Tip

You do not need to use the ICF if you are using a proxy server or another firewall. The ICF is intended for users who do not have any form of protection between their systems and the Internet or an external network.

1. On the desktop, right-click on **Network Neighborhood** and click **Properties**, shown in Figure 5.2.

Figure 5.2
Network Neighborhood options.

2. Double-click the connection using or requiring the ICF. See Figure 5.3.

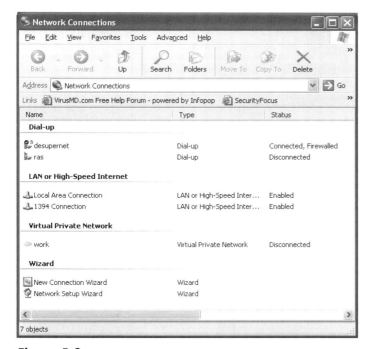

Figure 5.3
Network Connections window.

3. Click **Properties.** See Figure 5.4.

Figure 5.4
Dialup Connection properties
(Advanced).

4. Select the **Advanced** tab, shown in Figure 5.5.

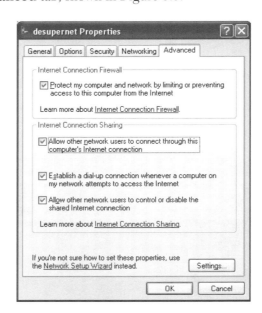

Figure 5.5
The Advanced tab.

5. To enable (or disable) the ICF, select (or deselect) the **Protect my computer and network by limiting or preventing access to this computer from the Internet** check box.

6. Click **OK** and then close the Dialup/Network connection dialog window.

The previous illustration will enable only the default settings of the ICF. This is adequate for some users, but these days even the average home user is adding services to their network (e.g., Napster, FTP Server). In the case that a computer owner needs to customize the settings of the ICF, the following will define and describe what settings can be adjusted and will describe the purpose of some of the settings.

Services Options

In the case that the ICF is enabled, but there are Web Services that need to be allowed to pass through the firewall, the default settings of the ICF are not acceptable. For situations like this, Microsoft has included the ability to allow data belonging to specific services to pass through the firewall. Not only does the ICF have the ability to enable or disable designated services, but it comes preloaded with a selection of the more typical Web Services that a user might need (Figure 5.6).

Figure 5.6
Advances Settings (Services).

Caution

Avoid enabling extra services unless they are necessary. Each service increases the chance of penetration.

The following defines each of the default services:

- FTP Server
  - Port: 21
  - Protocol: TCP
  - Purpose: The typical FTP server exists to hold files and provide Internet users with the ability to transfer files from server to client or vise versa.
  - Example: Microsoft uses an FTP server to host its free Web browser program (Internet Explorer) that the general public can download and install.
- Internet Mail Access Protocol Version 3 (IMAP3)
  - Port: 220
  - Protocol: TCP
  - Purpose: Software that allows users to retrieve email messages. Allows one user to access multiple mailboxes or folders on the Mail Server.
  - Example: Microsoft's Exchange Server
- Internet Mail Access Protocol Version 4 (IMAP4)
  - Port: 143
  - Protocol: TCP
  - Purpose: Software that allows users to retrieve email messages. Same as IMAP3, with the addition of new features such as search ability.
  - Example: Microsoft Exchange Server
- Internet Mail Server (SMTP)
  - Port: 25
  - Protocol: TCP
  - Purpose: Software that allows users to send email messages. Typically used by ISPs, an SMTP Email server is used by clients to send emails. Used in conjunction with POP3 Email server.
  - Example: Sendmail (°nix email program)
- Post-Office Protocol Version 3 (POP3)
  - Port: 110

100

- Protocol: TCP
- Purpose: Software that allows users to retrieve messages from one email account (folder) at a time. Used by businesses and ISPs in conjunction with SMTP server.
- Example: Sendmail (*nix email program)
- Remote Desktop
  - Port: 3389
  - Protocol: TCP
  - Purpose: Software used to allow a user to access their computer from a remote computer. Often used in work environments to allow users the ability to work from home.
  - Example: Microsoft's Remote Desktop Software
- Secure Web Server (HTTPS)
  - Port: 443
  - Protocol: TCP
  - Purpose: Software used to create a secure connection between client and host to pass sensitive data (e.g., credit cards, social security information) securely.
  - Example: An online store that uses SSL to encrypt the sales information sent from client to server.
- Telnet Server
  - Port: 23
  - Protocol: TCP
  - Purpose: Software used to allow one or more remote users access to a host computer. Typically used in *nix environments to provide users with the ability to work from home or remotely from the central server.
  - Example: Colleges often use Telnet servers to permit students access to email, programs, and other required information as their educational courses require.
- Web Server (HTTP)
  - Port: 80
  - Protocol: TCP
  - Purpose: Software used to package and ship Web pages from host computer to client computer.
  - Example: Microsoft's Internet Personal Web server software that is included, which is provided in all editions of Windows XP and will allow an owner to set up a personal Web site on their computer.

Adding a Service

If these options do not meet the requirements for a user's network, it is easy to add another. To illustrate, we will add an entry for an IRC (Internet Relay Chat) Server. This TCP-based program uses a default port of 6667.

1. Right-click on **Network Neighborhood** and click on **Properties**.
2. Right-click the connection using the ICF and select **Properties**.
3. Click on the **Advanced** tab and choose **Settings**.
4. Click on the **Services** tab.
5. Click **Add**.
6. Enter the following information (Figure 5.7):
   - **Description of service:** IRC Server
   - **Name or IP address of the computer hosting this service on your network:** IP address where IRC software is installed
   - **External port number for this service:** 6667
   - **Internal port number for this service:** 6667
   - Click **TCP**.
7. Click **OK**, **OK**, and then **OK** again to exit to the Network Connection window.

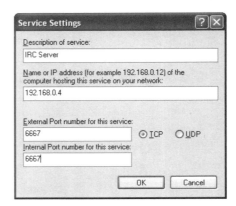

Figure 5.7
Adding IRC to ICF Services.

Editing and Deleting a Service

In the case that the Services settings need to be adjusted or deleted, the user can follow the instructions given under **Adding a Service**. However, instead of choosing the Add button on the Services window, a user should choose **Delete** or **Edit**. Once the Service has been changed, it will be saved when the user clicks **OK**.

Programs Options

This tab under ICF setting provides a user with the ability to allow designated programs to communicate through the firewall protection (Figure 5.8). Accounting programs, games, and any other Internet-based program will require an entry specifically defining the server port, client port range, and protocol that the program will use. You can usually obtain these by reading the manual or contacting the company responsible for the software.

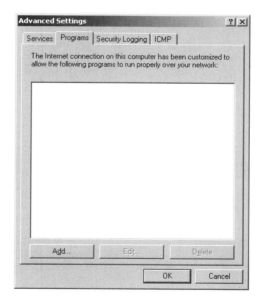

Figure 5.8
Program Options for the ICF.

While similar to the Services option in the ICF, the Programs option takes the ability to allow incoming requests for information one step further. Without this option, services could not work properly if installed on a computer inside the network. In fact, the Services used to pass through the ICF often require multiple ports to continue a session with a remote computer. This is to reduce the load on the one port defined by the Session definition and to instead pass the session to another port that can continue to accept data from a remote computer. For example, a Proxy Server typically receives the initial request for Web data on port 80 from a computer on the network and then passes the request to the destination on the Internet on a different port (i.e., 1032). The proxy server then accepts data back from the Internet on this port and passes it on to the requesting computer.

Adding a Program

To set up and use the Programs option built into the ICF, perform the following instructions:

1. Right-click on **Network Neighborhood** and click on **Properties**.
2. Right-click the connection using the ICF and select **Properties**.
3. Click on the **Advanced** tab and choose **Settings**.
4. Click the **Programs** tab.
5. Click **Add**.
6. Enter name of program under **Description of program running on your network**, shown in Figure 5.9.
7. Enter program port number under **Internet server port number**.
8. Enter the ports that the server should use to listen for responses from the Internet under the appropriate protocol (TCP, UDP) selection.
9. Click **OK**, **OK**, and **OK** again to exit back to **Network Neighborhood**.

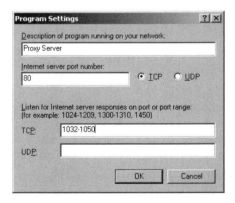

Figure 5.9
Adding Program to ICF.

Editing and Deleting a Program

In the case that a Program needs to be deleted or to have its settings adjusted, the user can follow the instructions given under **Adding a Program**. However, instead of choosing the Add button on the Program window, the user should choose **Delete** or **Edit**. Once the Program has been changed, it will be saved when the user clicks **OK**.

Security Logging Options

Proper logging is one of the most important elements of a secure server. With proper logging, tracking and repairing the outcome of a hack attempt and even a successful break-in can be as simple as viewing a log file and replacing the altered files. Without logging, the only way to verify that a server is secure is to reformat and reinstall the operating system and all programs running on the server.

Microsoft knows the importance of proper logging since they are one of the most frequently attacked companies on the Internet. Although disabled by default, the ICF has the ability to log all successful incoming connection requests, as well as those that are dropped. Used in combination with a properly configured server, a user can have a complete picture of activity on her computer. As a security rule of thumb, you should always enable logging. No other source of information can more clearly portray the actions of a hacker in the chance a computer is compromised.

There are two main subjects that need to be clearly understood in order to use the Security Logging feature of the ICF:

1. Setting and using Security Logging
2. Reading the results of Security Logging

The following segment will discuss each of these subjects and their importance to maintaining a secure computer system.

Setting Up Security Logging

As stated before, logging is one of the key parts of any secure system. However, the ICF Security Logging is disabled by default. The following steps will enable it:

1. Right-click on **Network Neighborhood** and click on **Properties**.
2. Right-click the connection using the ICF and select **Properties**.
3. Click on the **Advanced** tab and choose **Settings**.
4. Click the **Security Settings** tab.
5. Click the **Log dropped packets** and the **Log successful connections** check box. See Figure 5.10.
6. Change the location and name of the firewall log file under the **Name** text box.

 Tip

The last step in a professional hacker attack is to delete any trace of the attack. Since most users never change the location of the log files, it is a simple thing for a hacker to find and alter the log file to cover his tracks. If you move and rename the log file location, it becomes more difficult for the hacker to successfully cover his tracks. This also gives you an edge in removing any Trojan backdoors from a root kit. For these reasons it is highly recommended that you move the log file location.

7. Click **OK**, **OK**, and **OK** again.

 Tip

*To disable the Security Logging, simply ensure the **Log dropped packets** and **Log successful connections** options are unchecked.*

Figure 5.10
Security Logging setting of the ICF.

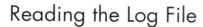

Reading the Log File

A log file can offer a wealth of information. However, the file is worthless if you cannot extract meaningful data. The following section analyzes a sample from an actual log file and explains the various parts.

```
1.  #Version: 1.0
2.  #Software: Microsoft Internet Connection Firewall
3.  #Time Format: Local
4.  #Fields: date time action protocol src-ip dst-ip src-port dst-port
    size tcpflags tcpsyn tcpack tcpwin icmptype icmpcode info
5.  2001-08-28 19:41:47 OPEN TCP 64.41.22.233 64.12.162.57 3555 5190 - -
    - - - - - -
6.  2001-08-28 19:41:48 OPEN TCP 64.41.22.233 205.188.8.12 3556 5190 - -
    - - - - - -
7.  2001-08-28 19:41:53 OPEN TCP 64.41.22.233 64.4.13.179 3557 80 - - - -
    - - - -
8.  2001-08-28 19:42:00 OPEN TCP 64.41.22.233 131.107.65.80 3559 80 - - -
    - - - - -
9.  2001-08-28 19:42:00 OPEN TCP 64.41.22.233 131.107.65.80 3560 80 - - -
    - - - - -
10. 2001-08-28 19:42:16 CLOSE TCP 64.41.22.233 64.12.162.57 3555 5190 - -
    - - - - - -
11. 2001-08-28 19:43:16 CLOSE UDP 64.41.22.233 207.69.188.187 3031 53 - -
    - - - - - -
```

Above is an excerpt of a log file taken from a dial-up computer over a period of a few seconds. In this example, you can see that the log file is full of numbers and other information. The key to understanding the data is found in the header of the file.

Line 4 contains the field names of each column of data. This makes importing the file into a spreadsheet application very easy. Figure 5.11 shows us the file as it appears after it is imported into MS Excel. Using this method of viewing, the information leaps out at us.

The following steps explain how to extract the information and import it into MS Excel.

1. Make a copy of the log file from its resident location to a temporary location.
2. Open the file and remove lines 1–3.
3. Remove the "#Fields:" from the left side of the new top line (previously line 4).
4. Open **Microsoft Excel** ➤ **Data** ➤ **Import External Data** ➤ **Import Data**.
5. Change **Files of Type** to **All Files (*.*)** and select the *.log file previously copied.

6. Choose **Delimited** and click **Next**.

7. Check the **Space** option.

8. Click **Finish** and **OK** to use the existing worksheet.

You should now have a window similar to Figure 5.12. The following will explain each field and its meaning.

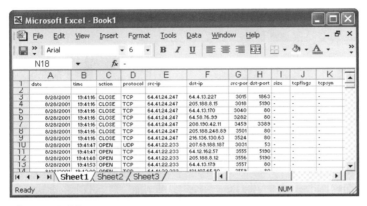

Figure 5.11
Viewing the ICF log file in Microsoft Excel.

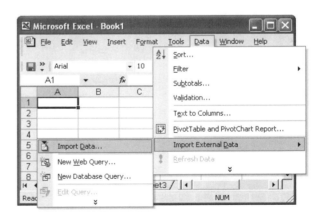

Figure 5.12
Using Microsoft Excel to import the log file.

- **Date**: Lists the date on which the connection attempt was made in YYYY-MM-DD format (e.g., 2002-02-05).

- **Time**: Lists the time that the connection attempt was made in HH:MM:SS format (24-hour format; e.g., 19:41:52).

- **Action**: Identifies the type of operation recorded by the ICF. The possible entries are OPEN, CLOSE, DROP, INFO-EVENTS-LOST. INFO-EVENTS-LOST is used when a number of actions occurred, but were not entered into the security log.
- **Protocol**: Identifies the protocol that was used for the connection attempt. While normally TCP, UDP, or ICMP will be entered, if an unknown protocol is used then a number representing the number of packets using the unknown protocol will be placed in this field instead.
- **Src-ip**: Identifies the source IP address from which the connection attempt originated (e.g., 192.168.0.4).
- **Dst-ip**: Identifies the destination IP address to which the connection attempt was made (e.g., 192.168.23.34).
- **Src-port**: Identifies the source port from which the connection attempt was made on the requesting computer. The entry will be an integer ranging from 1–65535. Only TCP and UDP will return a valid port number. If another protocol is used, port 4039 will be entered (e.g., 3023).
- **Dst-port**: Identifies the local port to which the connection attempt was made. The entry will be an integer ranging from 1–65535. Only TCP and UDP will return a valid port number. If another protocol is used, it will be entered (e.g., 80 is a common entry if the request is made to retrieve a Web page from the local host).
- **Size**: Identifies the size of the packet in bytes (e.g., 60).
- **Tcpflags**: Identifies the TCP control flag found in the header of all TCP packets. The flags are written as uppercase letters (e.g., ACK).
  - ACK—This flag says that the ack number is valid, which means that the sender is acknowledging the receipt of data.
  - FIN—This flag signifies that the sending end will not be sending anymore data.
  - PSH—This flag tells the receiving end to push all buffered data to the destination application. It essentially means there is no more data.
  - RST—This flag resets the receiving end of the TCP connection. Packets in error are replied to with this flag.
  - SYN—This flag is used to signify that both ends have to synchronize their TCP buffers.
  - URG—This flag is used to signify that the urgent pointer is valid and the data it refers to should be processed immediately.
- **Tcpsyn**: Identifies the sequence number used in a TCP session. This number is present when the tcpflag is set to SYN (e.g., 1315819885).

- ***Tcpack***: Identifies the acknowledgment number used in a TCP session. This number is present when the tcpflag is set to ACK. This number will be the next sequence number the local computer should expect to receive (e.g., 0).
- ***Tcpwin***: Identifies the TCP window size in bytes of the packet.
- ***Icmptype***: Identifies the number that represents the ICMP field Type (e.g., ICMP echo = 8).
- ***Icmpcode***: Identifies the number that represents the ICMP field Code. This number has various meanings depending on the ICMP type (e.g., Type = Destination Unreachable (3), Code = Host Unreachable (1)).
- ***Info***: Used as an extra entry to clarify an action that occurred. For example, an INFO-EVENTS-LOST action will record the number of events that happened but were not placed in the log since the last incidence of this type of event.

As you can see, the ICF Security log offers its users a wealth of information. Although it seems esoteric to many end users, this log can provide network administrators with proof of a hack attempt and its origin.

For example, one of the first things every hacker does against a target system is a port scan. If this is performed on a system with the ICF logging enabled, the attacker's IP address will show up in multiple entries over a brief period of time. In addition, if the hacker used a scanner that sequentially probes ports (e.g., 3045, 3046, 3047), the log file will be full of entries where the dst-port field increases by one. When used in conjunction with other logging options provided by Windows XP, the ICF log from end-user machines provides useful clues.

ICMP Options

Overview of ICMP

The Internet Control Message Protocol is one of the most common protocols used on the Internet. It is used for troubleshooting Internet connections, maintaining control, and gaining information about other computers. Defined in RFC 792, ICMP is the protocol used when computers and routers need to inform and control other routers and hosts on the Internet. Although a user or program usually generates the ICMP message, the response side is automated.

For example, the most popular usage of the ICMP protocol can be found in the program called PING. The Packet Internet Groper (PING) program is a very popular utility that is most commonly used to determine whether or not an IP address is in use or is available on the Internet and in local networks. Although many ISPs are restricting the use of the ICMP, and therefore PING, this program is still used by network technicians, hobbyists, Internet-based programs, and others who need to determine the status of others on the Internet. However, this group also includes hackers and other online criminals.

Hackers often use the ICMP protocol to determine whether or not targets are online and are even finding ways to abuse the protocol to crash computer systems. To prevent this from happening to home users, Microsoft has included an ICMP filter as part of the ICF. While a user can enable selected options of the ICMP filter, once the ICF is enabled, all connection attempts using the ICMP will be dropped. If Security Logging is in use, the packets will be logged and flagged as dropped.

Adjusting the ICMP Options

Making changes to the ICF's ICMP options is not to be taken lightly, especially if the network is a prime candidate for attack. Although each of the selections has a valid use, many are outdated and may not even be available from the Internet due to ISP regulations. However, on large networks that operate independently from the Internet, enabling ICMP may be necessary to assist network technicians with their duties. To enable ICMP options, observe the following instructions.

1. Right-click on **Network Neighborhood** and click on **Properties**.
2. Right-click the connection using the ICF and select **Properties**.
3. Click on the **Advanced** tab and choose **Settings**.
4. Click on the **ICMP** tab, shown in Figure 5.13.
5. Check the options you wish to have enabled.
6. Click **OK**, **OK** , and **OK** again, which will leave you at the **Network Neighborhood** window.

Understanding the ICMP Options

Before adjusting any of the options in the ICMP window, it is important to understand what impact it could have on your network and on the ability of hackers to learn information about the network/computer the ICF is protecting. For the average home user, there will not be a need to enable any of the ICMP options. However, for the corporate user, the need may arise to allow ICMP while restricting other connection attempts.

111

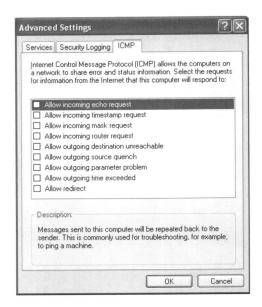

Figure 5.13
The ICMP options list in the ICF Advanced Settings window.

 Caution

Do not enable the ICMP options without a full understanding of the consequences. These options are required when a network technician needs to troubleshoot a connection. Immediately disable any option once the issue has been resolved.

The following will describe each of the ICMP options available to allow or disable.

Allow incoming echo request: This option controls whether or not a computer can reply to messages sent that ask for a response. PING is a program that would require this option to be enabled. However, if this option remains disabled, hackers would not be able to "see" the host computer.

Allow incoming timestamp request: The timestamp request is used to signal that a computer is listening to incoming requests by replying with the time/date that the signal was received.

Allow incoming mask request: This option of the ICMP is used to provide its requestor with the subnet mask of the target network. This information is useful for those who wish to connect to a network since this requires two components, namely the subnet mask and the IP address.

Allow incoming router request: This option supports the ability to pass on information to its requestor about any routers to which the host is connected. Since the Internet is a virtual Web of routers that are used to control the flow of traffic, each router builds a table of available paths that data can travel. To support this, a router must be able to communicate with other routers located in between itself and the destination.

Allow outgoing destination unreachable: This option supports the ability of a router inside the network to pass information back to the requestor about the status of a nonexistent or unreachable host.

Allow outgoing source quench: This option is available to allow routers and other bridging devices to inform the sender that too much data is being sent and to slow down. Although it is not commonly used since the reply messages slow down traffic even more, it is nevertheless one of the options of the ICMP.

Allow outgoing parameter problem: In case there is a problem with a connection that is not covered by any of the other ICMP reporting features, this option serves as the cover-all. When an error is encountered, the receiving computer replies to the client computer with a generic "bad header" response. If a hacker sent a malformed packet to a host, they would receive a response back, thus learning that the host exists.

Allow outgoing time exceeded: If the TTL (time-to-live) part of a packet's datagram is exceeded due to an excessively long data transfer time, the received information will be dumped and a message will be sent back to the original computer. Using this automated utility, a hacker could determine who was present on a network without raising alarms by using PING to query the existence of computers on a network.

Allow redirect: The redirect function of ICMP allows routers to correctly point data in the right direction. If a router sends information via the wrong path, the next intercepting router will send a "redirect" signal back to the originating router to correct its path table. This keeps data flowing efficiently on the Internet, but hackers could abuse it.

As you can see, the ICMP is responsible for many aspects of maintaining a healthy network. Router, host, and network technicians all use the ICMP to diagnose problems, make adjustments to router tables, and keep a watchful eye on where resources are located. However, hackers have been known to abuse the advantages offered by the ICMP; therefore, it is important to understand what can happen if it is re-enabled on a protected connection.

Internet Connection Sharing

Although not directly related to the ICF, the indirect relationship Internet Connection Sharing (ICS) has with the ICF warrants a segment in this chapter. This is because the ICF cannot be enabled on connections between client and host computers that are using the ICS. Although this is usually only on the internal part of a network, users who are not aware of how the ICS works may find that their connection to the Internet is wide open for attack or that their ICS will not work correctly.

The ICS is a two-part program that allows a network to require only one connection to the Internet, which is then shared with the rest of the computers on the internal network. The host part of the program runs on the computer that has the Internet connection, and the client part is installed on each computer that wishes to use the shared connection. In other words, the ICS acts as a proxy server that relays Internet requests from the network through one central computer. It also fields incoming requests for services on the network and passes them along to the appropriate destination. However, these services must be set up and enabled in the ICF in order for the connection to be successful.

Microsoft has many help files available for the proper setup and use of the ICS. For the most part, it is a fairly simple program without many options for the user. However, it is very important that a user understand the ramifications that setting up ICS can have on her network. For this reason, we have included the basic enable/disable instruction as a list (with explanation) of how the ICS affects a network.

Issues to Clarify before Enabling Internet Connection Sharing

Before turning on the ICS, the user must be cautious of how the ICS will adjust the settings of the local computer. It is also important to be aware of how enabling the ICS will interfere with other network services that may be required to stay connected to the network. For example, consider the following:

- The ICS will not work in networks using DHCP, other domain controllers, DNS Servers, or static IP networks. Because the ICS resets the host computer's IP address to 192.168.0.1 and becomes a DHCP server of its own, any other IP address managing servers on a network will be thwarted. This at a minimum will disconnect the local computer from the network and at most completely stop all communication on a network.
- When the ICS is enabled, all connections from the local computer will be broken. If the host computer is attempting to connect to the Internet when the ICS is enabled, or is querying another computer on the network, the connection will need to be refreshed. In the case that a network

connection cannot be reestablished, turn off the ICS and reevaluate the current IP addressing scheme used on the network.

- In order for clients to use the ICS, their IP address settings must be set to "automatic." In addition, clients must configure Internet options for Internet Connection Sharing to connect to the Internet.

Enabling/Adjusting/Disabling Internet Connection Sharing

Before enabling the ICS, ensure the previous issues are not applicable or are accounted for.

1. Right-click on **Network Neighborhood** and click on **Properties**.
2. Right-click the connection that you want to enable the ICS on and select **Properties**.
3. Select the **Advanced** tab.
4. Select the **Allow other network users to connect through this computer's Internet connection** check box in the **Internet Connection Sharing** frame.
5. In order for the connection to automatically dial upon an Internet request from the network, select the **Establish a dial-up connection whenever a computer on my network attempts to access the Internet** check box.
6. In order for other users on the network to control the status of the ICS, select the **Allow other network users to control or disable the shared Internet connection** check box.

Setting Up the Client for ICS

As previously mentioned, there are two parts to the ICS: the client and the host. We have already covered the host side; next we discuss the client side. Fortunately, setting up the client is a rather simple thing if everything on the host side was done properly. In fact, it can all be taken care of by running a simple program from a floppy on each client computer.

 Tip

   The Network Setup Wizard can only be run on computers using Windows 98, Windows 98 Second Edition, Windows Millennium Edition, or Windows XP.

To Create the Network Setup Client Disk

1. Start the Network Setup Wizard.
2. Follow the steps on your screen to configure your home or small office network. In order to correctly run the Network Setup Wizard:
   - **Host Name**—Desired name of host computer (if using cable modem, do not change the preexisting name without checking with the cable company).
   - **Workgroup Name**—Name of your network.
   - **Floppy Disk**—Used to create the Network Setup Client Disk.
3. When you come to the page that reads **You're almost done**, insert a blank, formatted floppy disk into the drive, and then click **Create Disk**.

To Run the Network Setup Program

1. Insert the network setup disk into the computer you want to network.
2. Double-click **My Computer**.
3. Double-click **3-1/2 Floppy (A:)**.
4. Double-click **netsetup.exe**.

Network Bridging

Network Bridging is another of the many enhancements that are new with Windows XP. This program gives its owner the ability to connect two segments of a network together easily and inexpensively. Although the average home user will never use this technology, the advanced or corporate user might. Traditionally, administrators needed extra hardware or specialized software to perform this task. In addition, with specialized software, the user would need to have a superior understanding of network routing protocols to successfully set up the network.

Network Bridging is an alternate solution that is as easy as selecting the two connections and selecting the Bridge Connections option. Not only does Windows XP take care of different media problems, it also takes care of converting different protocols, something that would have previously required costly equipment or advanced software settings.

Windows XP also uses the IEEE spanning tree algorithm (STA) to ensure that there are no loops created in complex networks. This ensures that if a network loops back on itself, data will not continue to travel around the network and clog the system.

Although the Network Bridge can be incredibly beneficial, it can also cause a serious security issue if it is enabled on the device used to connect to the Internet. This will give the world permission to access the internal network. For this reason, Windows XP makes it difficult to enable Network Bridging on an Internet connection. However, with the advent of high-speed connections and the increased use of Ethernet cards in these connections, it is entirely possible to bridge the Internet connection.

The following tips should be observed when enabling Network Bridging:

- In order to enable or disable network bridging, you must be logged in as an owner.
- You must have two qualified connections to create a Network Bridge.
- Only qualified adapters can be used to create a Network Bridge (IEEE-1394, Ethernet, Wireless, etc.).
- You can only create Network Bridges on Windows version XP and higher.
- You cannot create a Network Bridge on a connection using ICF or ICS.
- Only one Network Bridge can be created on a computer; however, the bridge can support unlimited connections.

Summary

The Internet Connection Firewall is an end user, integrated personal firewall whose rule set can be made as complicated or as simple as the user desires. With its default settings, a hacker will have a tougher time finding a way into the computer. In situations where more control and less restrictions are needed, the ICF can be set up to allow additional services, programs, and troubleshooting.

The ICF can also be used in conjunction with Internet Connection Sharing to keep a network of computers safe while permitting an Internet connection to be shared. While not adequate for corporate deployment, the ICF can handle most home users' networking requirements. However, the ICF will not protect against viruses, Trojans, or internal hackers intent on subverting the protection offered by the ICF. Network administrators should understand how the end user's ICF integrates with the enterprise security policy.

Chapter 6

WIRELESS SECURITY

This chapter covers:

- Overview of wireless networking
- Wireless authentication
- Setting up an automatic wireless network
- Connecting to an existing wireless network
- Using the wireless link
- Configuring wireless clients

Overview

One of the most significant trends in the telecommunication field is the rapidly expanding use of wireless networks. Wireless technology allows you to convert a network signal into a high-frequency radio wave. Through the use of compression and a wide range of frequencies, wireless networks have been able to exceed speeds of 54 MB/s. While not quite as fast as a tangible hard-wired network, which can reach 1,000 MB/s (using fiber), the home and business communities alike are enamoured of the concept.

Unfortunately, wireless networks have set the field of information security backwards by many years. For example, hackers routinely go "war driving," which involves driving through downtown and mapping the open wireless access points of large corporations. In this chapter, we introduce wireless networks and describe how to secure them on Windows XP.

Advantages of Wireless Networking

Wireless networks provide several advantages. For example, a wireless device does not require a physical wire connecting it to the rest of the network. In situations where the server is located in the next room, or across the street, going wireless can solve your connectivity problem. Similarly, wireless conference rooms or classrooms do not need individual wires running between each and every workstation.

Types of Wireless Networks

Wireless networks are similar to wire-based networks. The following provides a brief description of the different types:

- **WWAN:** The Wireless Wide Area Network is a public or private network of computer devices that exists over a large area, such as a city, state, or country. An example of these is the second-generation (2G) systems that are made up of cellular devices or other similar devices that have a low bandwidth requirement. Although this use is still in development, which makes it difficult to use due to lack of coverage and due to competing communication standards, there are plans for a 3G system that will help to eliminate these problems (unless 3G is usurped by the military). Another example of a WWAN was Ricochet, the wireless subscription-based ISP that was tested in many large cities in the United States. Although the business did not succeed, the concept was proven successful.

- **WMAN:** A Wireless Metropolitan Area Network is used to connect office buildings together over several blocks using radio frequency, microwaves, or infrared. Typically, this type of network is used as a backup in case the hardwired network fails or if a wireless connection is cost-effective compared to other options.

- **WLAN:** The Wireless Local Area Network is a confined network that typically exists within a building's walls. Used as an extension of the local network, the WLAN allows users to move about without losing their connection. Schools, businesses, and entertainment companies can use a WLAN to provide service to anyone with a wireless network card.

- **WPAN:** The Wireless Personal Area Network is a very localized (30 feet or less) network that allows devices to communicate directly with each other. Although the largest WPANs can expand to cover the range of a home or small business, they are typically confined to personal data assistants (PDAs) and other small devices that use infrared as their mode of data transfer.

Types of Wireless Connections

In addition to delineation by network topography, there are also different classes of wireless networks as defined by their connection type. These include the following:

- **Access point:** An access point is a central device through which several clients can connect and can access the network services. This can be a set of devices that act to route signals to and from clients, or it could be simply one device that limits its client to a short range. Typically, this requires that the client have a pass phrase to be permitted access. However, the pass phrase is not required and this could allow anyone with a wireless network card to access the network.

- **Computer to computer (ad hoc):** This type of wireless network is a simple connection between two devices. PDAs usually fall in to this category since they often pass files and other small amounts of information between each other. This type of network is most useful when only a temporary network is needed to pass data.

- **Access point/computer to computer combo:** In the case that a user requires flexibility, this is the suggested type of configuration. The computer will first search for any wireless access points and if none are found will use the ad hoc method of data transfer. An example of this is when a computer is part of a wireless network at work, but the computer also must be able to connect at home. This connection configuration will allow a user's computer to connect to whatever network is available.

The Wireless Link

Along with other new wireless features, Windows XP adds support for infrared. Infrared data transfer is not a new technology. Many remote controls, PDAs, and other small devices use this mechanism to transfer short bursts of data. Due to the 3-meter or less distance limitation, infrared is only used in situations where it is cost-effective or more efficient than a wired network.

However, since it is part of Windows XP we will make a brief mention of how to use it. The setup and configuration of a wireless link is simple. In fact, once an infrared device is detected as installed by XP, the operating system provides a link icon on the taskbar (Figure 6.1) and even presents a Wireless Link icon on the desktop (Figure 6.2) when another infrared device is within its vicinity.

Figure 6.1
Infrared device icon.

Figure 6.2
Infrared device present icon.

802.11 and 802.1x Authentication

Although wireless technologies have been around for some time, they only recently became popular. Now that the wireless network has become a cost-effective and practical addition to business and home networks, their use has spread exponentially. While this increase in market demand has forced vendors to create more streamlined and simple software and hardware solutions, this simplification has also made wireless networking a target for hackers.

802.11 Authentication

Vendors and network specialists have realized the weakness in wireless protocols and have attempted to build protection into the wireless network connection standard, known as *802.11*. However, this requires that the user understand and incorporate a pass phrase, encryption scheme, and more. Unfortunately, users do not always put security as their first priority. Because of this, many wireless networks are wide open to attack by anyone with a laptop. In fact, hackers (and security specialists) have learned that it only takes a few minutes of driving around a city with a laptop scanner to find a vulnerable network ("war driving").

The 802.11 standard permits a network to be made relatively secure if the user sets up her wireless network using WEP. (Although this standard has already been exploited, it has so far proven repairable.) The Wired Equivalent Privacy (WEP) algorithm is a collection of security services that, if used properly, protect the wireless network from being compromised. Due to the very nature of the wireless medium, that is, the air, it is a simple task for a device to "listen" to the data and grab sensitive information such as passwords. WEP consists of the previously mentioned pass phrase or encryption that uses secret, shared encryption keys that are generated by the host and then passed to the clients. These keys then alter the data that travels across the airwave, thus thwarting anyone using a sniffer on the network.

The two main types of authentication are properly known as:

1. **Open System:** The open system requires that the requesting station send its identification to the authenticating station, which either accepts or rejects the connection based on whether or not the identity is recognized.

2. **Shared Key:** The shared key system requires that a secret key is known by both the authenticating station and the requesting station. When a connection is attempted, the secret key is sent from the requesting station and is either accepted or rejected by the authentication station.

When Shared Key authentication is chosen, the user has the option to use the key to encrypt the data. As previously mentioned, this can protect sensitive data traveling across the wireless network from becoming captured. Since the key can be different lengths, the user is in control of how strong they want the encryption (40–104 bits). The bit strength corresponds logarithmically to how many guesses it would take to crack the code.

If a wireless network is using 802.11 authentication, the user can specify up to four different keys. Each key is assigned an index number (0–3). When data is passed from the requesting station to the authentication station, the index number is included and the authentication station uses the relative key to decipher the data.

Under 802.11, a wireless station can be configured with up to four keys (the key index values are 0, 1, 2, and 3). When an access point or a wireless station transmits an encrypted message using a key that is stored in a specific key index, the transmitted message indicates the key index that was used to encrypt the message body. The receiving access point or wireless station can then retrieve the key that is stored at the key index and use it to decode the encrypted message body.

However, even with the proper use of 802.11, including a strong password and encryption, hackers can capture the data. Although the details are outside the scope of this book, the weakness is found in the fact that the encryption scheme is predictable. With only a few hours of captured data, a savvy hacker can compromise a network. As a result, since Microsoft is genuinely concerned about our safety, they adopted the new, more secure 802.1x standard in Windows XP.

802.1x Authentication

802.1x takes its predecessor, 802.11, one step farther. Although it does support 802.11 authentication, 802.1x includes the ability to use computer and user identification, dynamic key creation, and centralized authentication. These extras make 802.1x more secure and eliminate many of the vulnerabilities of 802.11, according to leading industry developers (e.g., Microsoft and Cisco).

Included in the 802.1x standard is support for the Internet Authentication Service (IAS). IAS uses the Remote Authentication Dial-In Service (RADIUS) protocol, which turns the wireless access point into a client for a central RADIUS server that handles the connection request. If the connection is approved, the RADIUS server provides a unique key for *each new* wireless connection session. In addition, 802.1x supports the Extensible Authentication Protocol (EAP) that gives users the ability to use Smart Cards, certificates, the Message Digest 5 (MD5) encryption algorithm, and more as their method of authentication.

For example, using 802.1x authentication gives a hotel the power and the means to set up a wireless hotel that can allow patrons access to the Internet and their email, while keeping patrons from accessing private parts of the network or other guest computers. This assumes that each guest has a wireless network card in her computer, PDA, or Pocket PC and it is configured for such use.

Now that you understand the authentication that Microsoft built into Windows XP, you will have a better foundation for how to securely set up your wireless network. The following pages will illustrate how to set up and configure a wireless network.

Setting Up an Automatic Wireless Network

Setting up an automatic wireless network connection is a simple task because of the way Windows XP has integrated wireless technologies into the operating system. From setup to data transfer, Windows XP has integrated an easy yet secure method of communication into the networking software.

The first stage of setting up a wireless network is to acquire the hardware. Although a review of hardware appliances is beyond the scope of this book, all wireless networks consist of hosting access points and client network cards that are installed in desktop and mobile computers. The only exception to this is in the case of ad hoc networks in which two computers communicate directly with each other through wireless devices attached to the computer. Currently, there are several brands of wireless network devices on the market, all of which communicate at about the same speed (maximum 54 MB/s) over a 2.4-gigahertz connection using the same technology as the typical 900 mhz (.9 gigahertz) phone.

 Tip

Before purchasing any hardware to use with Windows XP, you should check to be sure it is on the compatibility list provided on the CD or at www.microsoft .com/hcl/default.asp.

In addition to compatible hardware, there are a few other requirements that must be met in order to use Windows XP's Wireless Connection settings. These include the following:

- You must be logged into the computer as an Administrator.
- The wireless adapter must support the Wireless Zero Configuration service. To verify this, check with your equipment representative or with the network adapter's manufacturer.

Once acceptable equipment is correctly installed on the computer using Windows XP, and all other requirements are met, it is time to make the connection and to configure the network settings.

1. Go to **Start**.
2. Right-click on **My Network Places** and select **Properties** from the menu.
3. Right-click the **Wireless Network Connection** and select **Properties**.

4. Select the **Wireless Network** tab.
   - Check the **Use Windows to configure my wireless network settings** box to enable automatic wireless network configuration. With automatic wireless network configuration enabled, you get:
     - Ability to connect to an existing wireless network
     - Ability to change wireless network connection settings
     - Ability to configure a new wireless network connection
     - Ability to set up preferred wireless networks
   - Clear the **Use Windows to configure my wireless network settings** box to disable automatic wireless network configuration. This option should be used if you are using third-party configuration software (e.g., WAP11 Configuration Software provided by Linksys with the wireless access point) or an unsupported network adapter.

Connecting to an Existing Wireless Network

 Tip

*At any time, click the **Refresh** button to reset the list of wireless networks within the range of your computer.*

Access Point Infrastructure and Ad Hoc Infrastructure

1. Click **Configure** under **Available Networks**.
2. Under **Wireless Network Properties**, denote the wireless network key settings, or select **The key is provided for me automatically** if the network adapter contains the settings. If there is any question about these settings, contact your network administrator or the wireless network adapter's manufacturer.

Access Point Special Note:
In the case that a network does not broadcast its name (i.e., DNS, WINS, and NetBIOS are not installed) the name will not appear under **Available networks**. To connect to a network that is available but not readily apparent, click **Add** under **Preferred networks**. In **Wireless Network Properties**, enter the network name (Service Set Identifier) and the WEP settings.

Ad Hoc Special Note:
In the case that both a computer-to-computer (ad hoc) network and access point (infrastructure) network are located within range of your computer and

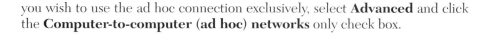

you wish to use the ad hoc connection exclusively, select **Advanced** and click the **Computer-to-computer (ad hoc) networks** only check box.

Changing the Wireless Connection Setting

1. Select the wireless network listed in Preferred networks that you wish to adjust.
2. Click **Properties** and alter the settings.

Configuring a New Wireless Connection

1. Under **Wireless Network Properties**, enter the **Service Set Identifier** as the network name, and, if necessary, the WEP settings.
2. If the new network is a computer-to-computer (ad hoc) network, check the **This is a computer-to-computer (ad hoc) network; wireless access points are not used** check box.
3. To enable your computer to automatically connect to networks within range that are not included on the **Preferred networks** list, select **Advanced** and then check the **Automatically connect to nonpreferred networks** box.

Adjusting the Preferred Wireless Connection

1. To adjust the preferred network list, click the wireless network you want to adjust, click **Properties**, and update the settings as required.
2. To delete a wireless network from the preferred network list, select the wireless network that you want to remove under **Preferred networks**, and click the **Remove** button.

The previous instructions will set up your wireless network under the 802.11 authentication method. To further secure your network, use the 802.1x authentication provided with Windows XP. The following segment will discuss this method in more detail.

Set Up 802.1x Authentication

802.1x authentication adds an extra level of security to the weak and vulnerable 802.11b authentication used by most wireless networks on the market today. Due to weaknesses in the Wired Equivalent Privacy (WEP) algorithm and issues surrounding misconfigured settings, sophisticated hackers or script kiddies with the right programs can gain access to a network in a few minutes. With the release of Windows XP, Microsoft puts added security in every user's grasp, with the one requirement that they have administrator permission. To set up the 802.1x security on a connection:

1. Go to **Start**.
2. Right-click on **My Network Places** and select **Properties** from the menu.
3. Right-click the **Wireless Network Connection** and select **Properties**.

 Tip

The ability to use 802.1x is available for all network connections, not just the Wireless Network Connection.

4. Click the Authentication tab, shown in Figure 6.3.
   - Check the **Enable network access control using IEEE 802.1X** check box to enable 802.1x authentication (enabled by default).
   - Clear the **Enable network access control using IEEE 802.1X** check box to disable 802.1x authentication.

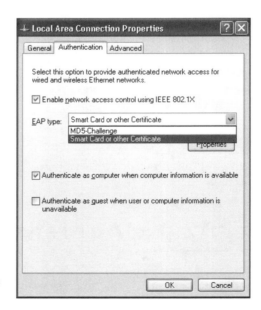

Figure 6.3
Connection Authentication Properties window.

5. Under **EAP type**, select the Extensible Authentication protocol you wish to use with the connection. If you use **Smart Card or other Certificate**, other options are available by clicking **Properties** and adjusting the **Smart Card or other Certificate Properties**, shown in Figure 6.4.

- To use the authentication provided by the certificate on your Smart Card, click **Use my smart card**.

- To use the authentication provided by the certificate stored on your computer, click **Use a certificate on this computer**.

- If using a certificate on the local computer:

  - Check the **Validate server certificate** box.

  - Select **Connect only if server name ends with,** enter the domain name, and select the **Trusted root certificate authority** from the drop-down menu.

  - Select **Use a different user name for the connection** if the Smart Card or local certificate does not contain proper information for the connection.

Figure 6.4
Smart Card or other Certificate Properties window.

6. To enable a computer to attempt authentication if the user is not logged on, select the **Authenticate as computer when computer information is available** check box.

7. To indicate that the computer should attempt authentication if authentication information is not available, check the **Authenticate as guest when user or computer information is unavailable** check box.

129

Connecting to Wireless Networks

Connection to a new wireless network is a simple thing in most cases in Windows XP. Typically, you will be alerted to a new available connection when an icon appears in the notification area next to the digital clock on the task bar. To access the wireless network, perform the following steps:

1. Right-click the network connection icon and click **View Available Wireless Networks**.
2. Under Available Networks in the **Connect to Wireless Network** window, select the desired wireless network.
3. Enter the required Wired Equivalent Privacy (WEP) information:
   - If the key is provided by the network adapter, leave the field blank.
   - If the key is not provided automatically, enter the requested WEP key.
4. Click the **Connect** button.
5. To adjust settings or troubleshoot the connection, select **Advanced** and alter the settings in the **Wireless Network** tab.

Summary

The wireless network is coming of age. Although still a bit expensive, within a short time wireless computing will be ubiquitous. By using the vulnerable 802.11 authentication method, users open themselves up to potential attacks. While the distance on PWANs limit the threat, larger corporations that use WWANs, WMANs, and WLANs may find their network compromised if they are not careful how the wireless leg of their networks are configured. To help mollify the security risks of WEP, Windows XP has included support for the new 802.1x standard, which includes the ability to require central authentication, dynamic WEP keys, and more.

Although the 802.1x authentication method is still under scrutiny, the Windows XP implementation of it helps to make wireless networking secure. In addition, Windows XP facilitates the initial setup and configuration of a wireless network into a simple wizard. By providing the user with a link icon and easily configured settings, Microsoft has enhanced the usability of its operating system.

Part IV

Configuring Windows .NET Server Security

4. The KDC on Domain 2 responds with a TGS for the network resource.

5. The client accesses the network resource on Domain 2 using the new TGS.

Changing Kerberos Default Policies

Kerberos can be fine-tuned for security in Windows .NET Server. For example, Kerberos has a *clock skew* feature that rejects ticket requests from any host whose clock is not within the specified maximum clock skew of the KDC. The default clock skew in Kerberos is 5 minutes. This feature is designed to prevent hackers from resetting their system clocks in order to continue to use expired tickets. In some cases, you may have to reduce maximum ticket lifetimes (for example, if your network is under heavy attack). All policy changes are enforced across the entire domain. This section will cover the steps involved in setting the Kerberos policies in Windows .NET Server.

The Kerberos policies available for configuration are as follows:

- Enforce user logon restrictions
- Maximum lifetime for service ticket
- Maximum lifetime for user ticket
- Maximum lifetime for user ticket renewal
- Maximum tolerance for computer clock synchronization

To configure Kerberos policies, perform the following steps:

1. Start the Active Directory Users and Computers MMC snap-in:
   - **Start ➤ Programs ➤ Administrative Tools ➤ Active Directory ➤ Users and Computers**
2. Right-click on the domain and select **Properties**.
3. Select the **Group Policy** tab.
4. Select the domain group policy object and click **Edit**.
5. Expand the Computer Configuration node:
   - **Computer Configuration\Windows Settings\Security Settings\Account Policies\Kerberos Policy**
6. Double-click the time you wish to change, modify, and click **OK**.

Figure 7.3 illustrates this process.

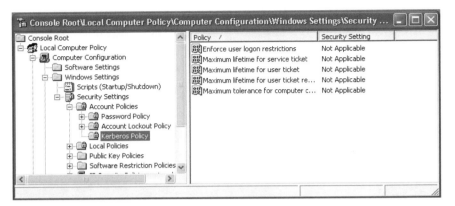

Figure 7.3
Configuring Kerberos policies.

Enforce User Logon Restrictions

This option determines whether the Kerberos v5 KDC authenticates every request for a session ticket based on the user rights policy of the target computer. By default, this setting is enabled in the Default Domain Group Policy object (GPO). Choosing to validate each request for a session ticket takes more time and may slow access to network services.

When this policy is enabled, the user requesting the session ticket must have the right to log on locally (if the requested service is running on the same computer) or the right to access this computer from the network (if the requested service is on a remote computer) to receive a session ticket. If this policy is disabled, the check is not performed.

Maximum Lifetime for Service Ticket

This allows you to set the maximum service ticket lifetime, specified in minutes. The default is 600 minutes (10 hours). After expiration, the user will have to renew the ticket. *Note*: Once the session is authenticated and established, it does not matter if the ticket expires; the ongoing service continues until the next request.

Maximum Lifetime for User Ticket

This option configures the maximum amount of time (in hours) that a user's TGT may be used. Interestingly, the setting is specified in hours, rather than in minutes as for the service ticket above.

Maximum Lifetime for User Ticket Renewal

This field determines the period of time (in days) during which a user's ticket-granting ticket (TGT) may be renewed. The default for this setting is seven days.

Maximum Tolerance for Computer Clock Synchronization

This specifies how accurately the network computer clocks must be synchronized. Lower numbers are more secure; the default is 5 minutes. See also "Clock Synchronization," below.

Kerberos Security Environment

Kerberos has numerous security advantages, but it is not a panacea. There are environmental security considerations that Kerberos cannot correct. In order for Kerberos to operate securely, it must be integrated with a well-designed, holistic security plan.

Some of the environmental variables and assumptions required for Kerberos to function properly are detailed in this section.

Application Attacks

Kerberos does not protect from DoS attacks. In addition, using reverse engineering or buffer overflows in the specific implementations, hackers can tie up system resources to the point of forcing the network to go down. This requires a watchful eye from a skilled system administrator.

Secret Keys

Another requirement of Kerberos is that principals must keep their secret keys secure. If a hacker steals a principal's key, he will be able to masquerade as that principal. He will also be able to spoof legitimate servers to the principal.

 Tip

Any key generation system should be in its own highly separate, secure realm. It should also have physical security for the server that stores the keys. Strict controls should exist on accessing this server with clear auditing trails on access.

Brute Force Password Attacks

Although Kerberos does not implement a defense against brute force password cracking, Microsoft's implementation does to some extent. That is why it is always important to implement preauthentication. In addition, it is of the utmost importance to enforce the choice of strong passwords. If the user's password is weak, a hacker can attack with a dictionary file by attempting to decrypt messages that are encrypted under a key derived from the user's password.

Any key generation system should be in its own highly separate, secure realm. It should also have physical security for the server that stores the keys. Strict controls should exist on accessing this server with clear auditing trails on access.

Clock Synchronization

Kerberos requires that the clock on each host on the network must be approximately synchronized to the time of the other hosts. The section on configuring Kerberos policy, above, describes the step for setting the degree of accuracy in synchronization. However, it is important to note that if the clocks are synchronized over the network, the clock synchronization protocol itself is vulnerable to hackers.

Kerberos Constants and Ticket Flags

KDC Constants

In a Kerberos implementation, the KDC should have the following constants or options in order to allow an administrator to make and enforce policy decisions:

- The minimum supported lifetime. This is based on reasonable expectations of round-trip time to the KDC, including time for encryption, decryption, and processing by the client and target server. It should allow for a minimum "useful" lifetime.
- The maximum allowable total (renewable) lifetime of a ticket.
- The maximum allowable lifetime of a ticket.
- Whether to allow the issue of tickets with empty address fields.
- Whether proxiable, forwardable, renewable, or postdatable tickets are to be issued.

Initial Tickets

The INITIAL flag indicates that a ticket was issued using the AS protocol and that it was not issued based on a Ticket-Granting Ticket (TGT). Setting this flag ensures that only tickets that were directly issued by the AS are accepted, because they are issued in direct response to the correct entering of a password, rather than use of the credentials cache. This is used in direct communications with a service. In addition, this flag is also set in a TGT issued directly by the AS. All tickets issued via the TGT have the INITIAL flag cleared.

Preauthenticated Tickets

The PRE-AUTHENT and HW-AUTHENT flags provide additional information about the initial authentication. This is regardless of whether the current ticket was issued directly, in which case the INITIAL flag will also be set, or issued indirectly on the basis of a TGT. When the PRE-AUTHENT flag is set, it provides validation to the AS that some authentication method was used before the initial ticket was issued.

The PRE-AUTHENT and HW-AUTHENT flags provide additional information about the initial authentication, regardless of whether the current ticket was issued directly (in which case INITIAL will also be set) or issued on the basis of a TGT (in which case the INITIAL flag is clear, but the PRE-AUTHENT and HW-AUTHENT flags are carried forward from the TGT). Moreover, if hardware authentication was completed through a Smart Card, which could only be utilized by the valid user, then the HW-AUTHENT flag is set.

As opposed to the INITIAL flag, the PRE-AUTHENT and HW-AUTHENT flags can be set in any ticket. Thus, if a ticket is not an initial ticket, then it inherits the values of these flags from the preceding TGT.

Invalid Tickets

Application servers reject tickets that have the INVALID flag set. An example of this is a postdated ticket. The KDC must validate INVALID tickets before they can be used. This is performed by presenting them to the KDC in a TGS request with the VALIDATE option specified.

Postdated Tickets

Suppose you want to run a batch application over the weekend, but you do not want to leave valid tickets sitting overnight in an online queue, because they might be stolen. In this case, you could issue a postdated ticket. The postdated ticket is inactive until it is authenticated by the KDC at the appropriate time. If a theft occurred in the interim, it could be reported and the KDC would subsequently refuse to validate the illicit ticket.

The TGT normally is responsible for interpreting the MAY-POSTDATE flag. Application servers do not process the flag. In order to issue a postdated ticket based on the presented ticket, this flag must be set in a TGT.

A TGT sent to the TGS may have the MAY-POSTDATE flag set to indicate that the TGS has the option of issuing a postdated ticket in response. This postdated ticket has the POSTDATED flag set. The client requests the MAY-POSTDATE flag by using the ALLOW-POSTDATE flag.

Renewable Tickets

In some cases an application may need tickets that are valid for longer periods of time. Unfortunately, this is a potential security risk. For example, a longer ticket life can expose credentials to hackers for longer periods. On the other hand, it is less secure to use a sequence of several tickets with shorter life spans. In this case, the client would have to have long-term access to its secret key, which is also a security risk.

A renewable ticket can help reduce the consequences of a stolen ticket. This is because renewable tickets have two expiration times. On the one hand, a renewable ticket expires when the current instance of the ticket expires. On the other hand, a renewable ticket will expire on the latest permissible value for an individual expiration time. Thus, the client must periodically present a renewed request to the KDC with the RENEW option set. The KDC will then respond with a new session key that has a later expiration time. This can continue until the latest permissible expiration time, at which point the ticket permanently expires. At each renewal, the KDC may check the ticket against a hot list of known stolen tickets and can refuse to honor illicit tickets. In this way, the effective lifetime of stolen tickets is reduced.

Proxy Tickets

If a client needs a service to obtain a ticket on its behalf, it can do so through use of a proxy ticket. In this way, the proxy service takes on the identity of the principal, but only for the particular purpose specified. This requires use of the PROXIABLE flag, which is normally interpreted by the TGS only.

The PROXIABLE flag is set by default. It allows a Ticket-Granting Server to issue a new ticket with a different network address. Thus, a client can send a proxy request to a server to perform a remote service on its behalf. However, as a security feature, Kerberos tickets are usually only valid from the network address specified in the ticket. Thus, the proxy flag allows a ticket (but not a TGT) to be issued with the network address of the service.

Forwarded Tickets

As opposed to proxy tickets, which give a remote service restricted client identity only, authentication forwarding provides a remote service full use of the client's identity. For example, this would permit a user to log into a remote system as if it were a local login. The flag allows for authentication forwarding without asking for a password again.

The FORWARDABLE flag is reset by default. It is interpreted like the PROXIABLE flag, except that in this case TGTs may also be issued with different network addresses. Thus, forwarded tickets are similar to proxy tickets, except that they can authorize the issuance of a TGT.

Interoperability with Other Kerberos Implementations

RFC-1510 (September 1993) describes the concepts and model upon which the Kerberos network authentication system is based. It also specifies version 5 of the Kerberos protocol. Windows .NET Kerberos v5 is designed for interoperability with other security services that are based on the RFC-1510 reference implementation. For example, a Windows .NET domain controller can provide authentication for client systems running implementations of RFC-1510 Kerberos, including clients running an operating system other than Windows XP Pro.

In addition, Windows XP Pro systems can authenticate to an RFC-1510 Kerberos server within a realm, with single sign-on to both the server and a local Windows XP Pro account.

Client applications for Win32 and operating systems other than XP that are based on the General Security Service Application Program Interface (GSS API) can obtain session tickets for services within a domain.

Public Key Cryptography and Kerberos

Public key cryptography is gaining increasing popularity. Advantages of public key cryptography in Kerberos would include simplified key management and the ability to utilize existing and developing public key certification infrastructures. Recently, efforts have been made to implement support for public key cryptography in Kerberos.

One Internet draft proposal for public key cryptography in Kerberos suggests associating a key pair with each realm, which can then be used to facilitate cross-realm authentication. Another proposal, RFC 1510bis (released July 2001) would allow users with public key certificates to use them in initial authentication.

The use of public key infrastructure (PKI) with Kerberos does change some security considerations. For example, PKI introduces a new trust model, where the KDCs themselves do not necessarily certify the identity of the client before granting tickets. Under PKI, KDCs can act as limited certificate authorities (CAs), but only when signing their own certificates. In addition, a PKI model can potentially cause varying levels of encryption strength within the model, which is a potential security weakness. Thus, system administrators who plan to adopt a PKI-based Kerberos implementation in the future should take care to become acquainted with the security vagaries of public key cryptography.

Summary

Kerberos is the default network authentication protocol in Windows .NET Server, and we recommend that you use it throughout your network. Kerberos is based on a system of tickets that provide mutual authentication from client to server and server to server. This chapter has shown you how to configure the security policies for Kerberos.

Secure use of Kerberos also requires a thorough understanding of the environment in which it is deployed. Always pay special attention to environments where there is a great deal of organizational change. Large turnover in users on the network is another thing to watch for when trying to keep security up to date.

Chapter 8

ENCRYPTING FILE SYSTEM

This chapter covers:

- What's different in the .NET Encrypting File System (EFS)
- Configuring the Data Recovery agent
- Using the command-line tool, Cipher.exe
- Working examples of the EFS
- Encrypting offline files

Overview

What's Different in the Windows .NET Encrypting File System

Windows .NET sports an updated version of the Encrypting File System (EFS) that was introduced in Windows 2000. File encryption is crucial because relying on default NTFS permissions is not enough. For example, hackers could load and boot into a different operating system on the same machine, thus potentially bypassing NTFS security. Moreover, a thief could steal a laptop and then extract data from the hard drive using forensic analysis tools.

Fortunately, however, the EFS provides built-in, transparent encryption for files and folders. Although the EFS is easy for Windows XP clients to use, as a .NET Server administrator you will want to master the intricacies of its protocol. This chapter shows you how to configure the EFS and recovery tools.

Windows .NET has enhanced its EFS since Windows 2000. For example, with Windows .NET you now have enhanced encryption of the offline files database. This is an improvement over Windows 2000, because cached files can now be encrypted. This chapter describes the Windows .NET EFS and will show you how to manage this powerful security feature.

Background

Microsoft's EFS is based on public key encryption and utilizes the operating system's CryptoAPI architecture. The EFS encrypts each file with a randomly generated key that is independent of a user's public/private key pair. The EFS automatically generates an encryption key pair and a certificate for a user if one does not exist. Temporary files are encrypted if the original file is on an NTFS volume. The EFS is built in to the operating system kernel and uses nonpaged memory to store file encryption keys so that they are never in the paging file.

In Windows .NET, encryption is performed using either the expanded Data Encryption Standard (DESX) or Triple-DES (3DES) algorithm. Both the RSA Base and RSA Enhanced software included by cryptographic service providers (CSPs) may be used for EFS certificates and for encryption of the symmetric encryption keys.

User Interaction

 Tip

Encryption works transparently for the Windows XP client, and users should be taught to utilize the EFS at all times for storing sensitive data. It is recommended to encrypt at the folder level to prevent plain-text temporary files from being left on the hard drive during the conversion.

The EFS supports file encryption on a per-file or per-folder basis. All child files and folders in an encrypted parent folder are encrypted by default. For simplicity, users should be encouraged to set one folder as encrypted, and to store all encrypted data in subfolders of the encrypted parent folder.

However, each file has a unique encryption key, which ensures that the file remains encrypted even if it moves to an unencrypted folder on the same volume.

 Caution

Moving an encrypted file from an NTFS volume to a FAT volume will decrypt the file. However, decryption will only occur if the user who encrypted the file is logged in when the file is moved.

Data Recovery

The File Encryption KEY (FEK)

Data recovery is a feature of the EFS that allows businesses to retrieve encrypted information. For example, if a user forgets his password, the default domain Administrator is able to decrypt and to rescue the encrypted files. Moreover, the default domain Administrator is able to delegate this decryption authority to other administrator accounts. This section will describe data recovery and will show you how to implement it in your security policy.

As mentioned above, the EFS uses public/private key pair cryptography. However, the public key does not encrypt the files themselves. Rather, each file has a unique key, called the *File Encryption Key (FEK)*, which is generated by the CryptoAPI. The public key in turn encrypts the unique FEK of each file. The FEK is stored in the Data Decryption Field (DDF) in the header of the encrypted file. Thus, when a user opens a file, the user's private key is used to decrypt the FEK. The FEK is then used to decrypt the file itself.

In addition, the public key of each recovery agent also encrypts the FEK separately. This recovery FEK is stored in a separate part of the header called the Data Recovery Field (DRF). Thus, when data recovery is used, the private key of the recovery agent decrypts its own FEK, which in turn decrypts the file.

If a Certificate Authority (CA) exists, the EFS will contact the CA for certification. However, the CA is not required. For example, on standalone machines, the EFS creates a key pair and self signs the certificate so that the user can get started using encryption without administrative configuration.

Recovering Encrypted Files

Configuring the Recovery Agent

By default, on a nondomain system the Administrator is the only recovery agent. However, when the machine is joined to a domain, the default domain Administrator account automatically becomes the default recovery agent.

To configure the recovery agent, first start the Active Directory Users and Computers MMC snap-in (as shown in Figure 8.1):

Start ➤ Programs ➤ Administrative Tools ➤ Active Directory ➤ Users and Computers

1. Right-click on the domain and select **Properties**.
2. Select the **Group Policy** tab.
3. Right-click the recovery policy you want to change, and then click **Edit**.
4. Expand the Computer Configuration tree to the following branch:

   - **Computer Configuration\Windows Settings\Security Settings\Public Key Policies\Encrypted Data Recovery Agents**

5. Right-click in the details pane to make changes.

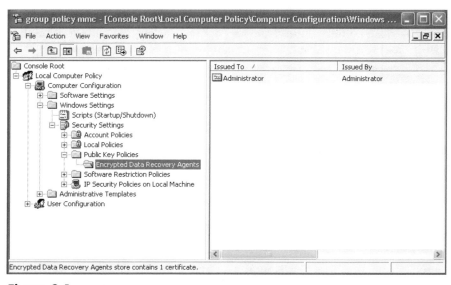

Figure 8.1
Active Directory Users and Computers MMC snap-in.

Figure 8.2
Add Recovery Agent Wizard.

Here you may change policies or add a recovery agent by right-clicking the **Encrypted Data Recovery Agents** node and selecting **Add**. This will bring up the Add Recovery Agent Wizard, as shown in Figure 8.2.

After changing policies or adding a new Recovery Agent, you may force an immediate refresh by using the following command-line instruction:

```
C:\> secedit /refreshpolicy machine_policy
```

Command-Line Recovery

EfsRecvr is a command-line utility that provides recovery agents with the ability to query recovery keys and recover an encrypted file, using any one of the recovery keys.

As an example, in order to recover all files in the **My Documents** directory, the recovery agent can type:

```
C:\>efsrecvr /s:"My Documents" *.*
```

The **efsrecvr** command can be configured with the following options:

```
EFSRECVR [/S[:dir]] [/I] [/Q] [filename [...]]
```

/S   Performs the recovery on files in the given directory and all subdi-
           rectories. Default "dir" is the current directory.

151

/I   Continues performing recovery even after errors have occurred. By default, EFSRECVR stops when an error is encountered.

/Q   Reports only the most essential information including the list of recovery key identifications to help the recovery agent load appropriate keys.

filename Specifies a pattern, file, or directory.

Using Cipher.exe

Cipher.exe is a command-line tool that allows you to do batch-encryption of files, folders, or subfolders. It is also useful if you want to find out which files on NTFS volumes are currently encrypted.

Syntax

The syntax for cipher.exe is as follows:

```
cipher [/e| /d] [/s:dir] [/a] [/i] [/f] [/q] [/h] [/k]
[/u[/n]] [PathName [...]]
```

Caution

Be very careful when using line commands for encryption. Always double-check your work before and after execution to ensure the command is having the desired effect.

Example

As an example, suppose you wanted to use cipher.exe to encrypt everything in a subfolder belonging to an engineer named Peikari in a parent folder named Software. The parameters for cipher.exe, listed below in the next section, specify that the **/e** option encrypts specified folders. Thus in order to encrypt just Peikari's folder, you would type the following:

```
cipher /e software\Peikari
```

However, suppose you wanted to encrypt not only Peikari's subfolder, but also the subfolders of all engineers in the Software department. For this you

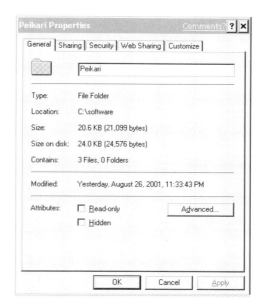

Figure 8.4
Encrypted Files Properties (General).

Figure 8.5
Advanced Attributes dialog box.

5. Click **OK** in the **Encrypted Files Properties** dialog box.
6. Next, you must choose between encrypting the folder and all of its contents or just encrypting the folder itself. Choose to encrypt the folder and all files and subfolders, as shown in Figure 8.6.
7. Click **OK** to complete the encryption.

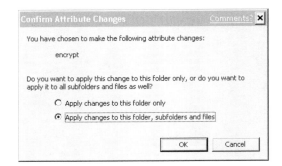

Figure 8.6
Confirm Attribute Changes.

  Caution

By using the EFS, users with higher rights may be able to decrypt your files and folders. Be sure to use encryption for legitimate work reasons only.

Decrypting a File or Folder

You can also use Windows Explorer to decrypt a folder or file. Recall that you do not need to decrypt a file to open the file and edit it—the EFS works transparently for the user. By formally decrypting a file, you are merely making it accessible to others.

You can decrypt a folder or file using Windows Explorer by performing the following steps:

1. Go to **Start ➤ Programs ➤ Accessories** and select **Windows Explorer**.
2. Right-click the folder or file name, and choose **Properties**.
3. On the **General** tab of the **Properties** dialog box, click **Advanced**.
4. On the **Advanced Attributes** dialog box, uncheck the **Encrypt contents to secure data** check box and click **OK**.
5. Click **OK** in the **Encrypted Files Properties** dialog box.
6. You are asked to choose between decrypting the folder and all its contents or just the folder itself. The default is to decrypt the folder only, and then click **OK**.

Using an Encrypted File or Folder

If you are the user who encrypted a file, you do not need to formally decrypt it before using it; the EFS operates transparently for this. You have the ability to open, edit, copy, and rename the file. However, if you are not the user who encrypted the file, you will receive an Access Denied error message if you attempt to access the file.

With an encrypted folder, if you had access to that folder before it was encrypted, you can still open it. When a folder attribute is set to "encrypted," it merely signifies that all files in the folder are to be encrypted as they are created; subfolders will also be marked encrypted at creation.

Copying an Encrypted File or Folder

Encryption is maintained when you copy a file or folder on the same computer from one NTFS partition in a Windows .NET location to another NTFS partition in a Windows .NET location. Thus, you can copy the file or folder as you would any unencrypted file. The copy will be encrypted. However, if you copy a file or folder on the same computer from an NTFS partition in a Windows .NET volume to a FAT partition, the file will lose encryption.

If you are copying a file or folder to a different computer where both use the NTFS partitions in Windows XP, encryption depends on the target computer. If the remote computer allows you to encrypt files, then the copy will be encrypted; otherwise it will be unencrypted. For the transfer to work, the remote computer must be trusted for delegation—in a domain environment, remote encryption is not enabled by default.

 Tip

After transferring an original from an encrypted file, check to make sure that the remote copy has remained encrypted. To do this, use the **File Properties ➤ Advanced** *option to confirm encryption on the destination file.*

Encrypted Files and Folders on a Remote Server

When logged in with the account that was used for the initial encryption, you can transparently encrypt, decrypt, and access files stored on a remote server. However, you must remember that when you move encrypted files using backup and restore mechanisms, you must ensure that the appropriate encryption certificate and private keys are also moved to allow you to use the encrypted files in their new destinations. Without correct private keys, you cannot open or decrypt the files.

 Caution

If you open the encrypted file over the network, the data that is transmitted over the network by this process is not encrypted. You must use other protocols, such as Secure Sockets Layer/Personal Communication Technology (SSL/PCT) or Internet Protocol Security (IPSec), to encrypt data over the wire.

Setting Up an Enterprise Certificate Authority

In order to set up an Enterprise CA, perform the following steps:

1. Log on to the first domain controller in the domain as the domain administrator.
2. Go to **Start** ➤ **Settings** ➤ **Control Panel**.
3. Double-click **Add/Remove Programs**.
4. Click **Add/Remove Windows Components**.
5. Click **Certificate Services**. You will receive a warning that once Certificate Services are installed, the computer cannot be renamed and the computer cannot join or be removed from a domain. Click **Yes** to continue. Click **Next**.
6. Make sure the **Enterprise root CA** radio button is selected and click **Next**, shown in Figure 8.7.
7. Fill in the properties and click **Next**.
8. Click **Next** to accept the default data storage location.
9. After the component has installed, click **Finish**. Close the **Add/Remove Programs** and **Control Panel**.

Encrypting Offline Files

Windows 2000 introduced a client-side caching functionality that in Windows .NET is now called *Offline Files*. This technology allows network users to access files on network shares even when the client computer is disconnected from the network. Mobile users can still browse, read, and edit files when disconnected from the network, because the data has been cached on the client computer. When the user later connects to the network, the system synchronizes the local changes on the server. Clients who use Windows XP Professional can thus use the EFS to encrypt offline files and folders.

Encrypting the Offline Files Database

Windows .NET now gives you the option to encrypt the Offline Files database. This is an improvement over Windows 2000, where the cached files could not be encrypted. System administrators can also use this feature to safeguard all locally cached documents. Encrypted offline files provides an additional level of security if your laptop or pocket PC is ever stolen.

This new feature supports the encryption and decryption of the entire offline database. In order to configure this option, you must be logged in as Administrator. To encrypt offline files, perform the following steps:

1. Open **Folder Options** under **Tools** in **My Computer.**
2. Check **Encrypt offline files to secure data** under the **Offline Files** tab. See Figure 8.13.

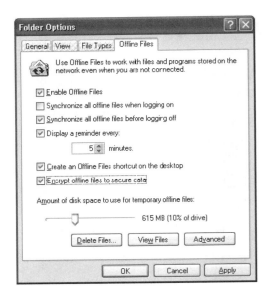

Figure 8.13
Folder Options.

Remote EFS Operations on File Shares and Web Folders

You have the option of encrypting remote files stored either on network file shares or on Web Distributed Authoring and Versioning (WebDAV) Web folders. Web folders are easier to manage and are more secure than file shares. Web folders also have the ability to securely store and deliver encrypted files over the Internet by using HTTP file transfers. The EFS manages this through Kerberos protocol delegation.

Remote EFS operations on files stored on file shares differ from operations on files stored on Web folders. When files are stored on file shares, EFS operations occur on the remote computer where the files are stored. For instance, if you connect to a network file share and attempt to open a file that you have previously encrypted, the file will be decrypted on the computer on which the file is stored; the data is then transmitted in plain text across the network.

In contrast, when you use Web folder storage, all EFS operations occur on your own local computer. For example, if you connect to a Web folder and choose to open a file that you previously encrypted, then the file remains encrypted during transmission; it is only decrypted when it reaches your local computer. Thus, Web folders are easier to use and are more secure than network shares.

Summary

The EFS provides built-in, transparent encryption for files and folders. New in Windows .NET is the offline file and folder encryption feature. In addition, the recovery agent allows you to reclaim data that has been scrambled by negligent or rogue employees. Administrators can also perform encryption using a command-line utility.

Chapter 9

PUBLIC KEY INFRASTRUCTURE

This chapter covers:

- Understanding PKI
- Benefits of Windows .NET PKI
- Deploying a Certification Authority
- Certificate Services backup and recovery

Overview

What is PKI?

Business networks no longer reside on isolated systems. The modern corporation draws its strength from the cultural diversity and innovation of its employees and partners scattered around the globe. However, this new "open" paradigm creates a much higher risk from hackers. Thus, there is now a corresponding need for stronger authentication.

Windows .NET answers this need with a set of services and administrative tools that are collectively known as "public key infrastructure." A *public key infrastructure* (PKI) is a system of digital certificates, certification authorities (CA), and other registration authorities that verify and authenticate the validity of each party involved in an electronic transaction through the use of *public key cryptography*.

In public key cryptography, the encryption and decryption keys are different. This is in contrast to symmetric key cryptography, where a single key is used for both encryption and decryption. In public key encryption, each user has a pair of keys, known as a *public key* and a *private key*. Public key encryption utilizes a one-way function to scramble data using the recipient's *public key*. The recipient must then use his private key to decrypt the data. This chapter shows you how to implement secure public key cryptography using the Windows .NET Public Key Infrastructure.

Common Public-Key Algorithms

In encryption applications, a tested and proven mathematical algorithm is almost always the strongest link in the security chain. Instead, hackers find other chinks in the armor, usually by exploiting weaknesses in the software packages (reverse engineering) or in their human operators (social engineering). Thus for most purposes, the encryption algorithm that you choose is actually the least important part.

However, advances in the field of quantum cryptography may soon reverse the situation. Using the semi-infinite power of molecular computing, it may soon be possible to effortlessly break encryption of any conceivable strength. For now, though, most algorithms are suitably strong. The following are some of the most commonly used and tested public-key algorithms:

- RSA—The algorithm is named after its three inventors, Ron Rivest, Adi Shamir, and Leonard Adleman. It is currently the most commonly used public-key algorithm. RSA is cryptographically strong and is based on the difficulty of factoring large numbers. RSA is also unique in that it is capable of both digital signature and key exchange operations.

- DSA—The United States National Security Agency (NSA) invented DSA (Digital Signature Algorithm). This algorithm can be used for digital signature operations, but not for data encryption. Its cryptographic strength is based on the difficulty of calculating discrete logarithms.

- Diffie-Hellman—Diffie-Hellman was named after its inventors Whitfield Diffie and Martin Hellman. This algorithm can be used for key exchange only. The cryptographic strength of Diffie-Hellman is based on the difficulty of calculating discrete logarithms in a finite field.

One-Way Hash Algorithms

A *hash* differs from key-based cryptography. A hash utilizes a one-way (irreversible) mathematical function (a *hash algorithm*) to transform data into a fixed-length digest, known as the *hash value*. Each hash value is unique. Thus, authentication using the hash value is similar to fingerprinting. To verify the origin of data, a recipient can decrypt the original hash and compare it to a second hash generated from the received message.

Two common one-way hash functions are MD5 and SHA-1. MD5 produces a 128-bit hash value and is now considered less secure. SHA-1 produces a 160-bit hash value. In PKI, hashes are used to create digital signatures.

Benefits of Windows .NET PKI

PKI is a combination of services that enable the use of public key cryptography. In Windows .NET, PKI is comprised by a set of operating system services and applications that allow you to implement a public key cryptography system of data exchange.

Although the infallibility of PKI is questioned from time to time, it nevertheless remains an important and growing part of information security. PKI can offer several benefits to your enterprise. These benefits include the following:

- **Data privacy:** By using strong encryption, PKI protects your enterprise communication on hostile public networks.

- **Authentication:** Because of the strength of the public–private key pair system, both the sender and the receiver can authenticate each other securely.

- **Strong security:** PKI integrates with Smart Cards (discussed in Chapter 10). Thus, when combined with Windows .NET IPSec (Chapter 14) and the Encrypting File System (Chapter 8), PKI becomes a powerful tool for maintaining data security.

- **Certificate management**: Administrators can use security permissions in Windows to determine what certificates can be issued to which users.

- **Simplified administration**: Administrators have the option to issue certificates instead of passwords. You can also revoke certificates as necessary and publish hot lists of banned certificates, known as certificate revocation lists (CRLs).

- **Scalability**: Certificate services are integrated with the Windows XP Active Directory and Group Policy. In addition, you have the capability to map certificates to user accounts via Internet Information Services. This provides great scalability for managing trust relationships across enterprises.

- **E-commerce security**: PKI provides the ability to implement secure e-mail using S/MIME (Secure Multipurpose Internet Mail Extensions) and secure Web connections using Secure Sockets Layer (SSL) or Transport Layer Security (TLS).

- **Nonrepudiation**: One of the most important advantages of PKI in electronic commerce is to establish *nonrepudiation* by the use of digital signatures. In other words, PKI allows you to prove that the person on the other end of the transaction actually made the purchase. Nonrepudiation means that through the use of digital signatures, the purchaser is unable to deny the transaction at a later date.

Certificate Authorities

Flavors of CAs

A Certificate Authority (CA) is any entity or service that issues *certificates*. CAs act as a guarantor of the binding between the public key and the owner's identity information that is contained in the certificates it issues.

This chapter will show you how to set up and configure your company's internal CA using Windows .NET Server. Windows .NET Certificate Authorities can be scaled to your enterprise size by using a system of CA hierarchies.

However, when you are using PKI in connection with commercial communications with outside organizations, you should consider outsourcing this service to a commercial CA. Their price varies depending on encryption strength and the level of service that you purchase.

 Tip

A trusted and cost-effective solution for securing enterprise infrastructure is VeriSign (www.verisign.com). The Verisign technology team is recognized as a leader in PKI.

An Issue of Trust

A *certificate* is a public key that is digitally signed and packaged for use in a PKI. Certificates provide the mechanism for establishing trust in a relationship between a public key and the owner of the corresponding private key.

A certificate will package a public key with a set of attributes relating to the key holder. For example, a certificate might contain the key holder's name, domain, and an expiration date.

When an authority issues a digital certificate, they are vouching for its accuracy. By issuing a certificate, the authority is testifying that the public key corresponds to the appropriate key holder. Thus, it is crucial that you trust the issuer of a certificate before you accept it.

In order to trust a CA, you must likewise have a certificate that attests to the CA and the binding between the CA and the CA's public key. However, this may require you to transitively verify the CA's certificate through a series of certificates ultimately linked to a central certificate that is known to be trusted; this central authority is called a *trusted root certificate*. Thus, the system relies on a chain of trust known as a *certificate chain*.

 Caution

Because of the hierarchical nature of CAs, if a trusted root certificate is hacked, then every certificate on chains leading to the root may be compromised.

X.509 Certificate Standard

Windows .NET uses the industry standard certificate format known as X.509 v3. X.509 specifies the certificate format for information about the person or entity to which the certificate is issued, information about the certificate, plus optional information about the certification authority issuing the certificate. Subject information may include the entity's name, the public key, the public-key algorithm, and an optional unique subject ID. Standard extensions for version 3 certificates accommodate information related to key identifiers, key usage, certificate policy, alternate names and attributes, certification path constraints, and enhancements for certificate revocation including revocation reasons and CRL partitioning by CA renewal.

Certificate Format

The standard format of X.509 certificates specifies the following components:

- **Version**: This specifies to which version of the standard (i.e., version 3) the certificate conforms.
- **Serial number**: Each certificate has a unique identification number.
- **Signature**: The digital signature of the CA which proves authenticity.
- **Issuer**: The name of the issuing CA.
- **Validity**: The start date and expiration date of the certificate.
- **Subject**: The certificate vouches for the pubic key of this user (subject).
- **Subject's public key information**: The value of the owner's public key.
- **Issuer unique identifier**: Another optional value to specify the unique owner.
- **Extensions**: Allow the certificate to be updated without requiring a new version of the standard.

Revocation

Certificates are normally issued with an expected validity period. However, certain circumstances may cause a certificate to become invalid prior to its expiration date. For example, if there is a known compromise of a corresponding private key, then the CA would have a need to revoke the certificate.

The X.509 standard provides for this revocation. This requires that each CA periodically issue a signed data structure called a certificate revocation list (CRL). The CRL is a time-stamped "hotlist" of invalid or stolen certificates that have been revoked. The revoked certificate's serial number is used to identify it in the CRL.

CAs issue new CRLs on a regular basis, which may be hourly, daily, or weekly. One advantage of this revocation method is that CRLs may be distributed through the same channels as the certificates themselves. However, one limitation of this method is that the "hotlist" of revoked certificates is only as current as the last periodic CRL issued by the CA.

Deploying a Certification Authority

Types of CAs

There are four basic types of CAs. The following section lists each type along with suggestions for when each would be most appropriate.

Enterprise Root CA—This is the root of a Windows .NET-based corporate CA hierarchy. In this scenario, the enterprise CA is typically configured to issue certificates only to subordinate CAs. An enterprise root CA utilizes Active Directory. It self-signs its own CA certificate.

Enterprise Subordinate CA—This CA is subordinate to another CA in the corporation's hierarchy. Enterprise subordinate CAs also utilize Active Directory and support Smart Card logon.

Standalone Root CA—A standalone root CA is a top-level CA in a certification hierarchy. The standalone root CA may or may not be a member of a domain and does not require Active Directory. This is typically used to issue certificates outside of your corporation's enterprise network. This allows you to give external parties certificate privileges without having to grant them access to your Active Directory. The certificates are usually issued to users through an intermediary standalone subordinate CA.

Standalone Subordinate CA—A standalone subordinate CA must obtain its CA certificate from another CA. The standalone subordinate CA may or may not be a member of a domain and, therefore, does not require Active Directory. This is the CA that issues certificates directly to users that are out of your enterprise network. The standalone subordinate CA usually derives certificates from the standalone root CA above it in the CA hierarchy.

Setting Up the Certificate Authority

Now that you have an understanding of the different types of CAs, you may proceed to configure your own CA. To set up a CA in Windows .NET, perform the following steps:

- Open **Control Panel ➤ Add/Remove Programs**
- Click **Add/Remove Windows Components** to start the Windows Components Wizard, shown in Figure 9.1.
- Select **Certificate Services** and click **Next**.

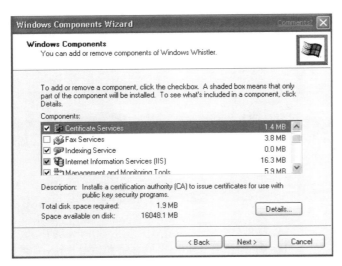

Figure 9.1
Windows Components Wizard (Add/Remove Windows Components).

- The Windows Component Wizard will ask you to select which type of CA you want to set up. Based on the "Types of CAs" section above, choose one that is most appropriate for your needs and click **Next** to continue. See Figure 9.2.

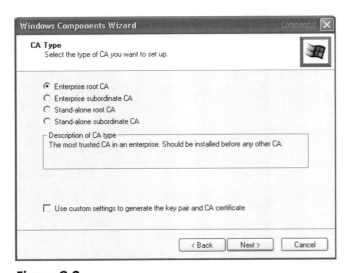

Figure 9.2
Windows Components Wizard (CA Types).

176

- The Wizard will prompt you to enter identifying information for your CA, including the validity period (default = 5 years). Fill in the fields and click **Next**.

- A dialog box specifies the locations of the certificate database and configuration information.

- Specify the storage locations for your data and finish the wizard based on your type of CA.

Custom Settings

If you choose to enable advanced options (by checking **Use Custom Settings**) when selecting the type of CA to install, you can select which cryptographic service provider (CSP) you wish to use. The CSP generates the public key and private key pair and performs cryptographic operations on behalf of the CA.

Under custom settings you can also set the key length for the public key cryptographic keys that the CA uses to sign certificates. Longer key lengths have the potential to be more secure. Setup requires more time to generate longer keys. You should choose a longer key length for protecting highly sensitive data.

In custom settings, you can also select which message hash algorithm is used by the CA. You can also choose to use existing cryptographic keys instead of generating new ones. See Figure 9.3.

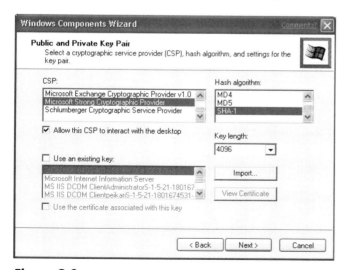

Figure 9.3
Windows Components Wizard (Public and Private Key Pair).

Database and Configuration Storage

Windows .NET Certificate Services uses local storage to maintain its database, configuration data, backup data, and logging data. You also have the option to specify locations for the database and log during CA setup.

The certificates issued by a CA are stored by default in the following location (Figure 9.4).

```
\Systemroot\system32\certlog
```

 Tip

You can also specify a shared folder when setting up your CA. This option is only useful if you are installing a standalone CA and do not have Active Directory. Instead, users can use the shared folder to find information about certification authorities.

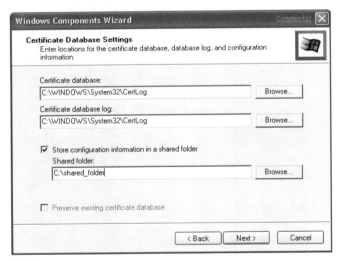

Figure 9.4
Windows Components Wizard (Certificate Database Settings).

Subordinate CAs

If you chose to install the enterprise subordinate CA, the host computer must be a member of a domain and must have Active Directory. If a parent CA is available online, perform the following steps:

- Select **Send the request directly to a CA already on the network.**
- Type the name of the parent CA computer in **Computer Name.**
- Click on the name of the parent CA.

However, if the parent CA is not available online, perform the following steps, as shown in Figure 9.5:

- Select **Save the request to a file.**
- In the **Request file** field, type the path and file name of the file that will store the request. The path must already exist.
- Obtain this subordinate CA's certificate from the parent CA.

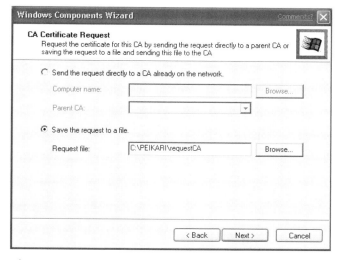

Figure 9.5
Windows Components Wizard (CA Certificate Request).

Renewing CA Certificates

You are able to renew a certificate while preserving its trust relationship. In order to renew a certificate, perform the following steps:

1. Open the Certification Authority Snap-In at the following location: **Start ➤ Programs ➤ Administrative Tools ➤ Certification Authority.**
2. Right-click the root CA and select **All Tasks ➤ Renew CA Certificate.**

Figure 9.6
Renew CA Certificate window.

3. The dialog box will prompt you to stop certificate services.
4. In the **Renew CA Certificate** window (Figure 9.6), choose whether or not you would like to generate a new public and private key pair. Generally, this will not be necessary.

Certificate Store

Creating a Certificates Snap-in

You can access a computer's certificate store using the Certificates snap-in. The snap-in is loaded by performing the following steps:

- Click **Start ➤ Run** and type **MMC** in the console. Click **OK**.
- On the console menu, select **Add/Remove Snap-In** and click **Add**.
- Select **Certificates** from the list of displayed snap-ins and click **Add**. See Figure 9.7.

After creating the snap-in, a dialog box (Figure 9.8) allows you to choose an account for certificate management. You can select the user account, service account, or computer account.

Figure 9.9 shows the completed snap-in.

Figure 9.7
Add Standalone Snap-in window.

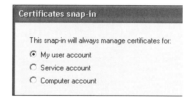

Figure 9.8
Certificates snap-in window.

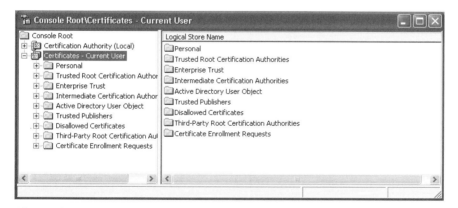

Figure 9.9
Completed snap-in.

You may select any certificate container to display a list of certificates for that store.

Installing the Certificate into a Store

To install a certificate into a store, perform the following steps:

- Right-click the store in which the certificate will be placed.
- Select **All Tasks ➤ Import** to start the Import Wizard, shown in Figure 9.10.
- Click **Next** to continue.
- In the **File to Import** dialog box shown in Figure 9.11, select the target file to import.
- Choose the Certificate Store in which to install.
- Click **Finish.**

Figure 9.10
Certificate Import Wizard.

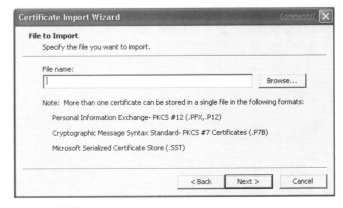

Figure 9.11
Certificate Import Wizard (File to Import).

Certificate Services Backup and Recovery

Backing Up Certificate Services

A crucial part of managing Certificate Services is providing for adequate backups. Ideally, the entire server should be backed with multiple redundant copies both locally and off-site as part of your enterprise backup and recovery plan. However, in cases when you do want a quick backup, you can locally store your CA using the steps outlined in this section. Using the Certificate Services backup tool, you can selectively back up keys, certificates, and the database, which includes a log of issued certificates and pending requests.

To back up Certificate Services, perform the following steps:

- Create a backup directory such as C:\BackupCA.
- Set permissions on the directory to allow access to the system and administrators only.
- Open the **Certification Authority** tool.
- Right-click the authority to back up and select **All Tasks ➤ Back up CA** from the drop-down menu, shown in Figure 9.12.

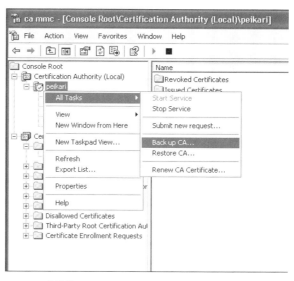

Figure 9.12
Certificate Authority tool.

This will cause the Certification Authority Backup Wizard to open, shown in Figure 9.13.

- Click **Next**. You will now be prompted to select which individual components you would like to back up. See Figure 9.14. Click **Next**.

Figure 9.13
Certification Authority Backup Wizard

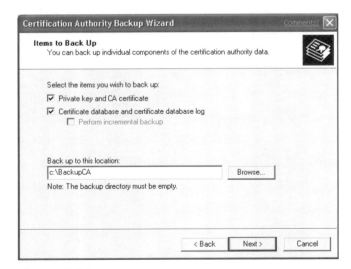

Figure 9.14
Certificate Authority Backup Wizard (Items to Back Up).

- You now need to select a password, shown in Figure 9.15.
- Click **Next** and then **Finish** to complete the Backup Wizard. See Figure 9.16.

You have now successfully completed backup of Certificate Services.

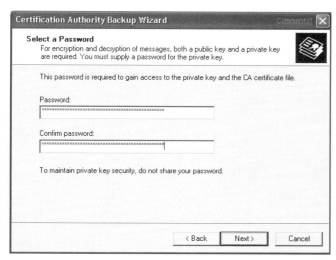

Figure 9.15
Certificate Authority Backup Wizard (Select a Password).

Figure 9.16
Certificate Authority Backup Wizard (Completing the Certification Authority Backup Wizard).

Restoring Certificate Services

If you need to restore Certificate Services from a backup, perform the following steps:

1. In the **Certificate Services** snap-in, right-click the CA.
2. Select **All Tasks ➤ Restore CA** from the drop-down menu.
3. You will be prompted to stop Certificate Services if it is running; do so.
4. The Certification Authority Restore Wizard opens, shown in Figure 9.17.
5. Select the items you wish to restore.
6. Browse to the backup directory and click **Next**.
7. Enter the password to access the private key and the CA certificate file.
8. Finish the Wizard.

Figure 9.17
Certification Authority Restore Wizard window.

Summary

Windows .NET supports PKI through a set of operating system services and applications that allow you to implement public key cryptography. Advantages of PKI include data privacy, authentication, strong security, and nonrepudiation. Windows .NET implements a standards-based PKI that supports a wide variety of PKI applications. Using Windows .NET, you can easily set up your own enterprise Certificate Authority and start issuing certificates, or you can outsource these services to commercial CAs.

Chapter 10

SMART CARDS

This chapter covers:

- Introduction to Smart Cards
- Deploying Smart Cards
- Choosing effective Smart Card reader hardware
- Configuring and using Smart Card authentication

Introduction

Smart Cards are one of the fastest growing sectors in information security. A *Smart Card* typically describes a plastic strip the size of a credit card that has an embedded microprocessor used for enhanced authentication. Windows .NET utilizes Smart Cards as an important component of the public-key infrastructure (PKI) that is integrated into the operating system. Smart Cards help secure software-based solutions such as interactive logon, client authentication, and remote logon. For the next few years, Smart Cards will be used at an accelerating rate.

Advantages that Smart Cards provide include:

- Tamper-resistant and permanent storage of private keys
- Physical isolation of secure private key computations from other parts of the system
- Ease of use and portability of credentials for mobile clients

Smart Card Specifications

The Smart Card does not have an internal power supply, but rather it becomes active only after insertion into a *Smart Card Reader*. Smart Cards come in various flavors, including stored-value cards, contact-less cards, and integrated circuit cards (ICCs).

The ICC is important in Windows .NET because it can perform complex calculations needed for digital signatures and key exchange. The specifications for contact-type ICCs are defined by the standard known as ISO/IEC 7816. Electrical contacts connected to various pins on the microprocessor chip are embedded in the surface of the plastic case such that an electrical connection can be made between an ICC Interface Device (IFD), also known as a "Smart Card reader," and the card itself.

Table 10.1 describes the use of each of the Smart Card's contacts.

Table 10.1. Smart Card Contacts

Contact	Designation	Use
C1	Vcc	Power connection through which operating power is supplied to the microprocessor chip in the card.
C2	RST	Reset line through which the IFD can signal to the Smart Card's microprocessor chip to initiate its reset sequence of instructions.
C3	CLK	Clock signal line through which a clock signal can be provided to the microprocessor chip. This line controls the operation speed and provides a common framework for data communication between the IFD and the ICC.
C4	RFU	Reserved for future use.
C5	GND	Ground line providing common electrical ground between the IFD and the ICC.
C6	Vpp	Programming power connection used to program EEPROM of first-generation ICCs.

Table 10.1. Smart Card Contacts (Continued)

Contact	Designation	Use
C7	I/O	Input/Output line that provides a half-duplex communication channel between the reader and the Smart Card.
C8	RFU	Reserved for future use.

Smart Card Authentication

A Smart Card communicates with applications running on its client computer via a half-duplex serial interface. The Smart Card reader and its device driver control the serial interface.

A Smart Card authenticates to the Windows .NET Server domain in one of the following ways:

1. An interactive logon utilizing Active Directory, the Kerberos version 5 protocol, and public key certificates.
2. Client authentication using a public key certificate matching an Active Directory account.
3. Remote logon using a public key certificate with the Extensible Authentication Protocol (EAP) and Transport Layer Security (TLS) to authenticate a client to a matching Active Directory account.

Interactive Logon

A client performs Interactive Logon by inserting a Smart Card into a Windows XP Professional machine. Card insertion has the same effect as using Ctrl-Alt-Del to initiate a password-based logon. However, in this case the software will detect the card and will prompt the client for a Personal Identification Number (PIN) instead of a username, domain name, and password. The other difference is that the PIN the user provides to the logon dialog is used to authenticate only to the Smart Card and not to the domain itself. The Smart Card stores a public key certificate that uses an extension to the Kerberos version 5 protocol to authenticate. (Chapter 7 describes the Kerberos authentication protocol in detail.)

 Caution

Remind users that they should never write their PIN numbers on their Smart Cards.

Client Authentication

Windows .NET supports the Smart Card reader directly through the CryptoAPI. Because of this, the Smart Card operates transparently to the Secure Sockets Layer (SSL) and Transport Layer Security (TLS) protocols. In client authentication, the role of the Smart Card is only to sign a part of the protocol during the initial SSL session negotiation. Because the private key corresponding to the public key certificate is stored on the Smart Card, the method of authentication is stronger because use of the private key requires the holder of the card to authenticate to the card and to the domain.

Remote Logon

Windows .NET includes a built-in module for Smart Cards to enable strong authentication for remote users. Remote logon involves two separate authentications. The first authentication result certifies the client and establishes communication to the RAS server. The second authentication is to the domain and uses EAP over TLS instead of Kerberos or standard SSL as the authentication protocol. The authentication to the domain over EAP/TLS is similar to client authentication using SSL, except that the public key certificate must match an account stored in the domain's Active Directory.

Deploying Smart Cards

Properly used, Smart Cards can help your corporation save money. On the one hand, Smart Cards provide strong network authentication, which can help reduce damage incurred by nonprofessional hackers. On the other hand, Smart Cards allow corporations to manage their own certificate services, which prevents costly outsourcing solutions.

Issuing Smart Cards

Once your corporation has decided to deploy Smart Cards, the cards themselves should be issued to general employees that are usually members of the Windows .NET User's profile. General users do not perform advanced or administrative network tasks, and hence they can use Smart Cards instead of passwords. Passwords are expensive and difficult to manage, and Smart Cards help reduce this administrative burden.

However, members of the Power Users or Administrators group should not rely on the use of Smart Cards only. For example, Administrators need to perform advanced tasks such as joining a computer to a domain, promoting a server to be a domain controller, or configuring a network connection for remote access. In this case, an Administrator password provides unrestricted access to the system.

Smart Card Policies

Public key security policy is integrated into Windows .NET and is described in Chapter 9. In addition, the following section describes several types of policies that system administrators can set to control the use of Smart Cards within a Windows .NET Server domain.

Smart Card Required

Windows .NET provides an account policy known as "Smart Card required for interactive logon" that can be configured on a per-user basis. This policy requires that the user present a Smart Card in order to initiate an interactive logon. This policy effectively prevents the user from logging in with a password, either interactively or from a command line. Although this policy applies to interactive and network logon, it does not change remote access logon which uses a different policy configured on the remote access server. It is recommended that you set a Smart Card required for interactive logon policy for those users who are members of the Users group that are using Smart Cards to log on to a Windows .NET Server domain.

The Smart Card required for interactive logon policy is not recommended for users who are required to join a computer to a domain or for those users who must perform administrative tasks such as promoting a server to be a domain controller or configuring a network connection for remote access. In these cases, the user will need to provide a username, domain name, and password because these are advanced administrative tasks that do not support using public key-based authentication.

On Smart Card Removal

When users walk away from a computer with an active logon session, they are expected to either log off or lock the computer. If the user fails to do this, then the screensaver program could lock the computer if it is configured to activate after a brief period of inactivity. However, while the session is active and open, a rogue employee could walk up to the unattended machine and cause damage.

This policy is recommended in situations where users interact with computers in an open floor or kiosk environment. In situations where users have dedicated computer(s) that only they use, a screensaver program could be used instead of this policy.

Left Card at Home

One situation that occurs frequently is when employees that have a long commute leave their Smart Card at home. In this situation, one option is to issue a temporary Smart Card with a certificate that has a short expiration such as 24 hours. Another option is a temporary password. In this case, you would not set the Smart Card required for interactive logon policy; instead, give the employee a long password that is used for that day only and is subsequently reset. The more sadistic network administrator will prefer to send the employee home to retrieve his Smart Card.

 Caution

Balancing convenience with security is always difficult. However, as an Administrator you must develop an effective policy for people who forget or lose their cards, or else chaos will reign. Users must bear some responsibility for their Smart Cards. Always get the backing of management on such a policy.

Personal Identification Numbers

One advantage of Smart Cards is that they use PINs instead of passwords. PINs do not have to follow the same rules as "strong passwords" because the cards are less susceptible to brute force dictionary attacks. A short PIN is secure because an uncompromised Smart Card will lock when too many wrong PIN inputs are attempted in a row. Furthermore, the PIN itself is never transmitted over the network, so it is protected from classic sniffing attacks.

Unlike a password policy, it is not necessary to change the PIN frequently. In fact, there is no change-PIN functionality available through the standard desktop logon interface as there is for passwords. This is because the change-PIN capability is only exposed to the user when a private key operation is being performed. This is due to the lack of standards for how PINs are managed across card operating systems, thus preventing PIN management from being done at the operating system layer.

Windows .NET-Certified Readers

Smart Card readers come in a variety of types depending on the application. Windows XP Pro clients support industry-standard, Personal Computer/Smart Card (PC/SC)-compliant Smart Cards and plug-and-play Smart Card readers that conform to specifications developed by the PC/SC Workgroup. To function with Windows XP Pro, a Smart Card must conform physically and electronically to ISO 7816-1, 7816-2, and 7816-3 standards. Smart Card readers attach to standard personal computer peripheral interfaces such as RS-232, PC Card, and Universal Serial Bus (USB). Some RS-232 readers have an extra cable that plugs into the PS/2 port to draw power for the reader.

To help customers determine which Smart Card readers are compatible with the Windows platform, Microsoft has developed a logo program for Smart Card readers, administered by the Windows Hardware Quality Lab, to ensure computer compatibility and card and reader interoperability. The Smart Card logo program is similar to what Microsoft has done for many other device types such as sound cards, network cards, and graphics cards. The advantage of this program is that you can purchase readers that have the Windows-compatible logo and you can rest assured that the device meets all of the requirements for compatibility and interoperability, including device driver quality, power management, and plug and play.

Table 10.2 lists all Smart Card readers that were certified by Microsoft as Windows XP compatible at the time of this writing.

Table 10.2. Smart Card Readers Certified to be Compatible with Windows XP

Manufacturer	Product Number
O2Micro Inc	OZ773
American Express	American Express GCR435 USB
BULL	BULL SmarTLP3 Serial

195

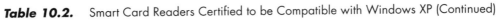

Table 10.2. Smart Card Readers Certified to be Compatible with Windows XP (Continued)

Manufacturer	Product Number
GEMPLUS	GEMPLUS GCR410P Serial
GEMPLUS	GEMPLUS GemPC430 USB
GEMPLUS	GEMPLUS GPR400 PCMCIA
Hagiwara	Compact Flash
Hagiwara	Flashgate SmartMedia R/W [USB]
HP	HP ProtectTools Serial
Litronic	Litronic 220 Serial
Omnikey AG	Omnikey AG CardMan 2010 Serial
Omnikey AG	Omnikey AG CardMan 2020 USB
Omnikey AG	Omnikey AG CardMan 4000 PCMCIA
SanDisk	Compact Flash
Schlumberger	Schlumberger Reflex 20 PCMCIA
Schlumberger	Schlumberger Reflex 72 Serial
Schlumberger	Schlumberger Reflex Lite Serial
SCM Microsystems	SCM Microsystems SCR111 Serial
SCM Microsystems	SCM Microsystems SCR120 PCMCIA
SCM Microsystems	SCM Microsystems SCR200 Serial
SCM Microsystems	SCM Microsystems SCR300 USB
Systemneeds	Systemneeds External Serial

 Tip

You can always find the updated list of Windows XP Pro-compatible Smart Card readers under the Smart Card Reader section at the following URL: www.microsoft.com/hwtest/hcl

Smart Card Reader Design

Interface Device

The Smart Card reader, or Interface Device (IFD), is a PC peripheral that:

- Interfaces to an ICC.
- Supports bidirectional data communications between an ICC and a PC.
- Incorporates the functionality required to support the interface exposed by the IFD Handler (described below).

Interface Devices must be designed for physical compatibility with the ICC interface.

I/O Channel

An I/O channel allows the IFD Subsystem (described below) to communicate with the IFD. Each Smart Card vendor creates specific IFD Handler and device drivers as necessary to ensure that the ICC Service Providers can communicate with the ICC through the Interface Device. The IFD vendor must provide appropriate management services and error handling related to the PC I/O channel to ensure reliable, error-free communication.

The following is a list of different designs for the PC I/O channel:

- *PS/2 Keyboard Integrated Interface Device*. This is a low-cost solution for handling Smart Card I/O. This is currently the most popular solution for desktop PCs because of ubiquitous PS/2 keyboard interfaces. However, this design's major drawback is the maximum data rate limit of 9600 bps and potential impact in keyboard response.
- *Serial Port (RS-232C) interface*. Serial ports can easily support multiple data rates, including support for rates in excess of 30 kB/s, and are suitable for use with desktop and laptop PCs. However, this design's major drawback is the relative dearth of serial ports on most PCs.
- *PC Card-based Interface Devices*. PC card devices are more expensive, but they do offer the best solution for retrofitting existing laptop PCs.
- *USB interface*. USB interfaces provide a great deal of flexibility, capacity for multiple devices, and high data rates. The major drawback is the absence of USB interfaces on older PCs.

The IFD Subsystem

The IFD Subsystem, defined in the standard ISO 7816 layer definition, as a whole, is responsible for the implementation of the Physical and Data Link layers. Figure 10.1 depicts the flow of information between the ICC Service Provider and the IFD Subsystem. The IFD Subsystem hides all protocol-related details from the application level and presents a standard interface based on ISO 7816-4 commands/responses structure.

An "IFD Subsystem" consists of the following elements:

1. An Interface Device (IFD), which provides the ICC interface
2. An I/O channel managed by an I/O device driver on the PC side
3. PC-hosted IFD handler software

The PC-hosted IFD handler software interfaces with the upper layer of the system architecture and the low-level I/O device drivers, as depicted in Figure 10.1.

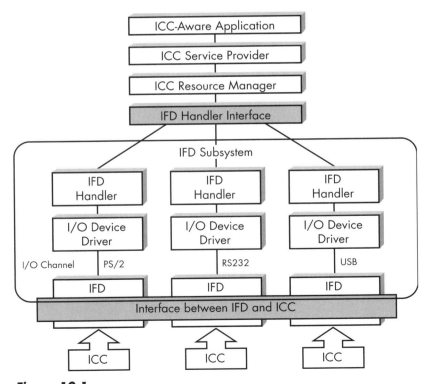

Figure 10.1
IFD System Architecture.

The IFD Subsystem employs a layered architecture, which allows for design variations and supports a variety of data communications interfaces between the Interface Device and PC.

The IFD Handler

The IFD Handler is software running on the PC that implements a standard, hardware-independent, and I/O channel–independent interface into the IFD subsystem for PC-based software. The IFD Handler's job is to interface to the I/O channel used by the Interface Device through device drivers (Figure 10.2).

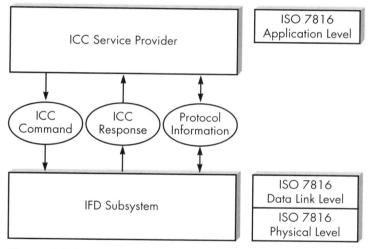

Figure 10.2
Role of the IFD Handler in terms of the ISO 7816 layers.

Configuring the Smart Card Reader

Smart Card readers should be installed on the Windows XP Professional workstation. Although you should follow the specific instructions of each manufacturer, the following is a generic list of instructions for configuring the Smart Card reader.

Connecting a Desktop Smart Card Reader

In order to connect a Smart Card reader, perform the following general steps:

1. Shut down and unplug the computer from the wall.
2. Attach the reader to an available serial port. For PCMCIA devices, insert the PC Card reader into an available PCMCIA Type II slot.
3. If your serial reader has a supplementary PS/2 cable/connector, attach your keyboard or mouse connector to it, and plug it into your computer's keyboard or mouse port. Many new Smart Card readers take power from keyboard or mouse ports because RS-232 ports do not always provide it and it is both expensive and cumbersome to require a separate power supply.
4. Boot your machine and log on as a user with administrative privileges.

Installing a Smart Card Reader Device Driver

If the Smart Card reader has been detected and installed, the **Welcome to Windows** logon screen will acknowledge this. If not:

1. Follow the onscreen directions for installing the device driver software.
2. Right-click the **My Computer** icon on your desktop, and click **Manage** on the submenu.
3. Expand the **Services and Applications** node, and click **Services**.
4. In the right pane, right-click **Smart Card**. Click **Properties** on the submenu.
5. On the **General** tab, select **Automatic** in the Startup Type drop-down list, as shown in Figure 10.3. Click **OK**.
6. Reboot your machine if the Hardware wizard instructs you to do so.

If the Hardware wizard does not start automatically, then your Smart Card reader is not a plug-and-play device.

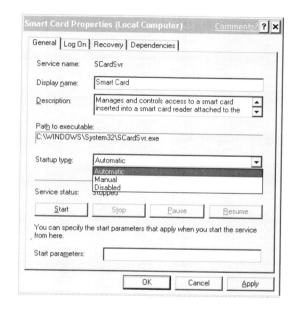

Figure 10.3
Smart Card Properties (Local
Computer).

Smart Card Certificates

Configuring the Certification Authority for Smart Cards

In order to prepare a certification authority to issue Smart Card certificates, perform the following steps:

1. Confirm that the proper security permissions are set on the **Smart Card Logon**, **Smart Card User**, and **Enrollment Agent** certificate templates.
2. Log on with Administrator rights to the CA you will be using to issue Smart Card certificates.
3. Open **Start ➤ Programs ➤ Administrative Tools ➤ Certification Authority**.
4. In the console tree, click **Certificate Templates**.
5. On the **Action** menu, point to **New**, and then click **Certificate to Issue**.
6. Click the **Smart Card Logon** certificate template, and then click **OK**.

Smart Card Certificate Enrollment

A domain user cannot enroll for a Smart Card Logon (authentication) or Smart Card User (authentication plus email) certificate unless a system administrator has granted the user access rights to the Certificate Template stored in the Windows .NET Active Directory. This is done to control physical access in the same way that employee badges are controlled. Microsoft recommends that users be enrolled for Smart Card-based certificates and keys through a Windows enrollment station.

When an Enterprise Certification Authority (CA) is installed, the installation includes the enrollment station. This station allows an administrator to act on behalf of a specific user to request and install a Smart Card Logon or Smart Card User certificate onto the user's Smart Card. The enrollment station does not provide any card-personalization functions, such as creating a file structure or setting of the PIN, because those are card-specific functions and can only be performed using specialized software provided by the Smart Card manufacturer.

The following steps show you how to enroll for a Smart Card Logon or Smart Card User certificate on behalf of a specific user.

1. Double-click the **Microsoft Internet Explorer** icon on the desktop.

2. To connect to a Certification Authority, type **http://machine-name/ certsrv** into the Address field of Microsoft Internet Explorer (where machine-name is replaced with the name of the computer running the issuing Certification Authority).

3. The **Microsoft Certificate Services Welcome** page appears. Select **Request a certificate**, and then click **Next**.

4. The **Choose Request Type** page appears. Select **Advanced request**, and then click **Next**.

5. The **Advanced Certificate Requests** page appears. Select **Request a certificate for a Smart Card on behalf of another user** using the **Smart Card Enrollment Station**, and click **Next**.

6. The very first time you use the Smart Card Enrollment Station, a digitally signed Microsoft ActiveX control is downloaded from the Certification Authority server to the enrollment station computer. To use the enrollment station, select **Yes** in the **Security Warning** dialog box to install the control.

7. The **Smart Card Enrollment Station** page appears. On this page, you must do the following before submitting a certificate request on behalf of another user: Select either the **Smart Card Logon** or **Smart Card User Certificate** template. Select a Certification Authority. Select a Crypto-

graphic Service Provider. Select an Administrator Signing Certificate. Select the **User To Enroll**.

8. Complete the first three items by selecting each item from the drop-down list boxes on the **Smart Card Enrollment Station** page.

9. After selecting the Certificate Template, Certification Authority, and Cryptographic Service Provider, select the Administrator Signing Certificate by clicking **Select Certificate**. A dialog box appears, showing a list of certificates that can be used. Choose only one certificate from the list (if more than one certificate is displayed), then click **OK**. Optionally, you can view the certificate by clicking **View Certificate**. Clicking **Cancel** results in no certificate being selected.

10. Select the user who is being enrolled for the certificate. Click **Select User**. Click **OK** to complete.

11. You are now ready to submit the certificate request. Click **Enroll**.

12. If the target Smart Card is not already in the Smart Card reader, a dialog box appears, prompting you to insert the requested Smart Card. Once the card is inserted into the Smart Card reader, click the **Retry** button.

13. As part of the certificate enrollment procedure, the request must be digitally signed by the private key that corresponds to the public key included in the certificate request. Because the private key is stored on the Smart Card, the digital signature requires that the signer of the request authenticate the card to ensure that the signer is the owner of the Smart Card (and, by extension, of the private key). Type in the PIN for the card, and then click **OK**.

Summary

Smart Cards are one of the fastest growing sectors in information security. Smart Cards can form an important part of security through PKI. Windows .NET makes it easier to deploy Smart Cards in your organization. By using the Smart Card readers listed in this chapter, you can be sure that they will be certified by Microsoft to be compatible.

Chapter 11

DESIGNING SECURE
VIRTUAL PRIVATE NETWORKS (VPN)

This chapter covers:

- How to create and configure a secure VPN using Windows .NET
- VPN protocol security and encryption
- VPN packet filters
- RADIUS security features on Windows .NET

Overview

At one point, it was widely assumed that as long as you had a firewall on each end of a transmission, your data was safe. However, by using packet sniffers, hackers have painfully and repeatedly shown this to be false. Virtual Private Networks (VPN) address this dilemma by creating fully encrypted channels to protect data. VPNs take full advantage of the power of the Internet by creating secure, private networks contained within hostile, public networks. VPNs are one of the fastest growing sectors in information security; over two-thirds of businesses are predicted to implement VPNs over the next few years.

An IT definition of a *VPN* is a solution for transmitting data over a network using a combination of tunneling, encryption, authentication, and access control. Microsoft has further generalized the term by defining it as a method of providing security across a public or untrusted network infrastructure. By integrating IPSec with its Active Directory service, Microsoft created the first operating system-integrated, end-to-end VPN solution. This chapter focuses on building VPN solutions for security using Windows .NET Server. In addition, this chapter introduces the new features of RADIUS servers (described below) that are introduced in Windows .NET Server.

Key Features of VPNs

- Encrypt traffic either between two points or two entire networks
- Usually software-based (rather than hardware-based)
- Provide variable levels of encryption, militated largely by export restrictions

Background

A VPN allows you to establish a secure, encrypted network within a hostile, public network such as the Internet. VPNs provide several benefits, including the following:

Benefits of VPNs

- Facilitate secure and easy interoffice communication
- Provide inexpensive network access for mobile employees
- Provide full network access for telecommuters

For example, VPNs are useful if you are traveling with a laptop, Pocket PC, or wireless smartphone and you need to access your company's network. A VPN will allow you to connect to your company from anywhere in the world through an inexpensive, local Internet connection.

VPNs are also useful for international companies with branch offices in different countries. Using local connections, your company can become globally and securely networked over the public Internet.

VPNs provide secure, encrypted communication in two ways:

1. *User-to-network (remote-access model)*—In this configuration, remote clients may connect through a public network such as the Internet. By using a VPN, the remote client can become part of the company network. This

configuration effectively replaces the remote dial-in or authenticated firewall access model.

2. *Network-to-network (site-to-site model)*—In this configuration, one branch office network may connect through a public network such as the Internet to another branch office network. This configuration obviates the need for an expensive wide area network (WAN).

Thus, VPNs are secure communication solutions that take advantage of public networks to lower your costs. However, VPNs are not without their share of problems. Some challenges involved in establishing VPNs are as follows:

Challenges facing VPNs

- Connection recovery
- Scalability of traffic and users
- User management and client deployment
- Speed
- Uptime
- Global interoperability
- Intrusion Detection System (IDS) encryption conflicts

 Caution

Experience has shown that even VPNs are not 100% secure. Consider having an outside, third-party security audit of your test VPN network before live deployment. The results may surprise you.

VPN Protocols

Two main protocols that have evolved for use in VPNs include the following:

1. *PPTP (Point-to-Point Tunneling Protocol)*—This is Microsoft's protocol for VPNs. It was designed to provide authenticated and encrypted communications without requiring a public key infrastructure. PPTP uses a TCP connection for tunnel maintenance and Generic Routing Encapsulation (GRE)-encapsulated PPP frames for tunneled data. PPTP is less common than the popular industry-standard Internet Protocol Security (IPSec), described next.

207

2. *Internet Protocol Security (IPSec)*—IPSec (Chapter 14) delivers machine-level authentication and encryption for VPNs based on L2TP (Layer 2 Tunneling Protocol). IPSec provides integrity protection, authentication, and optional privacy and replay protection services. It is an architecture protocol and related Internet Key Exchange (IKE) protocol, which is defined by IETF RFCs 2401–2409. The IPSec packets comprise the following types:

- IP Protocol 50: This is the Encapsulating Security Payload (ESP) format. It defines privacy, authenticity, and integrity.

- IP Protocol 51: This is the Authentication Header (AH) format. It defines authenticity and integrity, but not privacy.

IPSec utilizes encryption based on either DES (Data Encryption Standard), which is 56 bits, or 3DES (Triple DES), which is 3 x 56 or 168 bits in strength. The maximum bit strength allowed for export by the U.S. government is militated by the part of the world in which the VPN server or client resides. Thus, it is common to have mixed encryption strengths within a single VPN, which can be a potential security weakness.

IPSec can work in two modes: *transport mode* and *tunnel mode*. Transport mode secures an existing IP packet from source to destination, while tunnel mode places the packet into a new IP packet that is sent to a tunnel endpoint in the IPSec format. Both modes allow encapsulation in ESP or AH headers.

Windows IP Security

The Windows .NET implementation of IPSec is known as Windows IP Security. Windows .NET Server integrates IPSec architecture with Active Directory. Using RFC Protocol 2409, the IETF-defined Internet Key Exchange (IKE) protocol provides security negotiation and key management. IKE provides the following authentication methods:

1. Kerberos 5.0 authentication

2. Public/private key signatures using certificates

3. Preshared authentication keys (passwords)

Because it so important, we have included an entire chapter on Windows .NET IPSec (Chapter 14). The rest of this chapter will walk you through the steps involved in configuring a secure VPN server.

Configuring the VPN Server

In order to configure a VPN, you should be logged into the machine that will run as a VPN Server. Then, under **Administrative Tools**, select **Routing and Remote Access**. Select **Add Server** on the **Action** menu and then select **This Computer**. See Figure 11.1.

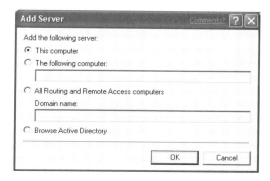

Figure 11.1
Add Server window.

VPN Configuration Wizard

Next, right-click the server and select **Configure and Enable Routing and Remote Access**. As for most functions in Windows .NET Server, a convenient wizard helps you set up the VPN. Start the wizard and select the **Virtual Private Network (VPN) server**, as shown in Figure 11.2.

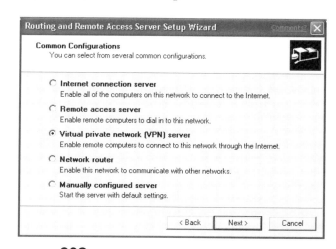

Figure 11.2
Routing and Remote Access Server Setup Wizard.

You will next be presented with a dialog box asking you to select remote client protocols. If you have all the necessary protocols installed, you can proceed. If not, you may need to install the required protocols on the machine. To do this, you must first go to

Start ➤ Settings ➤ Network and Dial-up Connections

And select **Make new connection**.

VPN Packet Filtering

Once you have the necessary protocols installed, you may proceed with the wizard. The next dialog allows you to filter traffic selectively for VPN packets only.

 Tip

To maximize security, apply the VPN filters if you are using this machine exclusively as a VPN server.

To filter packets for VPN traffic only, click the option that says **Yes, create VPN-only packet filters for this server**. The next dialog asks you to select IP address assignment. You can assign IP addresses to clients either automatically or from a specified list of addresses.

RADIUS

You will next be asked to specify if you would like the current server to utilize an existing Remote Authentication Dial-in User Service (RADIUS) server (Figure 11.3). RADIUS is an industry standard protocol defined by RFCs 2138 and 2139 that provides authentication, authorization, and accounting services for distributed dial-up networking (see "RADIUS features" below).

Once you have finished the wizard, you will get a notice asking you to configure your DHCP relay agent. To do this, expand the Routing and Remote access tree. Right-click on the node for "DHCP Relay Agent" and select **Properties**. You can now enter the IP address of your DHCP server.

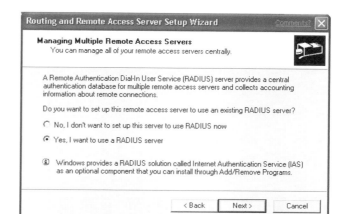

Figure 11.3
Routing and Remote Access Server
Setup Wizard (Managing Multiple
Remote Access Servers).

Configuring the VPN Client

Installing the VPN client

The steps for installing a PPTP VPN client using Windows XP Pro are somewhat different from Windows 2000. To install the VPN client on Windows XP Pro, go to

Start ➤ Settings ➤ Network and Dial-up Connections

and select **Make New Connection**. A friendly wizard will open, shown in Figure 11.4.

Figure 11.4
Network Connection Wizard.

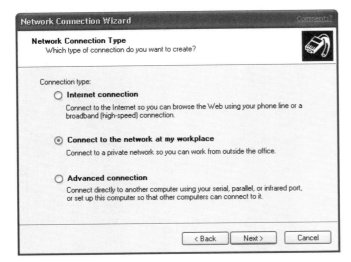

Figure 11.5
Network Connection Wizard (Network Connection Type).

You will next need to select **Connect to the network at my workplace**, and then in the dialog screen shown in Figure 11.5, select **Virtual Private Network**.

In the next dialog screen, shown in Figure 11.6, enter the destination IP address to which you are connecting.

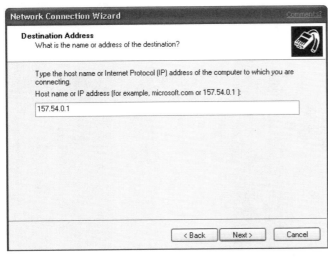

Figure 11.6
Network Connection Wizard (Destination Address).

Caution

> *Avoid placing your VPN server name in DNS. For security reasons, always use the IP address only.*

New RADIUS Features in Windows .NET Server

A RADIUS server uses the Internet Authentication Service (IAS) to provide authentication and accounting support to networks that have multiple RRAS and VPN servers. Windows .NET Server introduces new features for RADIUS servers. These include the RADIUS proxy, wireless authentication support, and authenticating switch support. The following section briefly describes these new features.

RADIUS Proxy

Windows .NET includes RADIUS proxy support in addition to RADIUS server support. Because of RADIUS proxy support, IAS can act as a RADIUS request router or forwarder. In this configuration, the RADIUS proxy forwards the RADIUS message to a specific RADIUS server for additional processing.

IAS implements RADIUS proxy support through connection request processing and remote RADIUS server groups. When a connection request is processed, it is either authenticated and authorized by the IAS server (when the IAS server is acting in a RADIUS server capacity), or it is forwarded to another RADIUS server for authentication and authorization (when the IAS server is acting in a RADIUS proxy capacity). When acting as a proxy, IAS forwards the connection request to one of the possible configured multiple remote RADIUS server groups.

Thus, an IAS server can selectively act as a RADIUS server for some requests and a RADIUS proxy for others.

Wireless Authentication Support

Windows .NET Server continues Microsoft's trend toward adopting industry standards in its new implementation of wireless protocols IEEE 802.11 and 802.11b. This standard attempts to address pervasive security problems in wireless networks. For example, attackers who have compatible wireless network adapters can gain access to a network. Furthermore, wireless networks use radio waves to transfer data. Thus, anyone within a few hundred feet of a wireless access point can intercept all data sent to and from the wireless access point. (Wireless security is covered in detail in Chapter 6.)

In order to counter these security risks, IAS supports wireless access authentication by supporting the Extensible Authentication Protocol-Transport Level Security (EAP-TLS). This protocol provides computer certificate-based authentication and determination of Microsoft Point-to-Point Encryption (MPPE) keys used to encrypt data sent between WAPs and wireless nodes. Furthermore, IAS supports the use of 802.11 port types when configuring the "NAS-Port-Type" condition of remote access policies. By using these port types, you can create a separate remote access policy that contains connection parameters and encryption settings specifically designed for wireless nodes.

Authenticating Switch Support

Network switches provide selective filtering of traffic and allow optimized traffic management by segmenting a network. However, switches send and receive packets without discrimination, which can be a problem for switch ports in a conference room of an organization. In this case, a malicious user from a competing organization could simply connect her network adapter to the switch port to gain instant access to your network.

To counter this, recent switches are RADIUS clients and use the industry standard RADIUS protocol to send connection requests and accounting messages to a central RADIUS server. The RADIUS server has access to a user account database and a set of rules for granting authorization. The RADIUS server processes the switch's connection request and either grants the connection request or rejects it.

IAS supports switch access authentication by supporting EAP-TLS to provide computer certificate-based authentication. Furthermore, by using the "Ethernet" port type, you can create a separate remote access policy that contains connection parameters specifically designed for switch nodes.

Configuring a RADIUS Server

To configure your RADIUS server, you must be logged into your IIS server. First make sure that IAS is installed. Go to

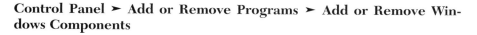

Control Panel ➤ Add or Remove Programs ➤ Add or Remove Windows Components

and make sure that Networking Services are installed. Then, go to

Administrative Tools ➤ Internet Authentication Service

Next, right-click on **Internet Authentication Service** and select **Properties**. Click on the **Service** tab and check both logging options, as shown in Figure 11.7.

Then, click on the RADIUS tab and specify the RADIUS authentication and accounting UDP ports to be used. Then, in the console tree, right-click on the **Clients** node and select **New Client**. The wizard will allow you to configure each RADIUS client. See Figure 11.8.

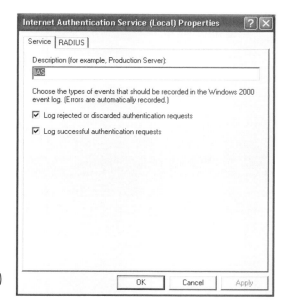

Figure 11.7
Internet Authentication Service (Local) Properties.

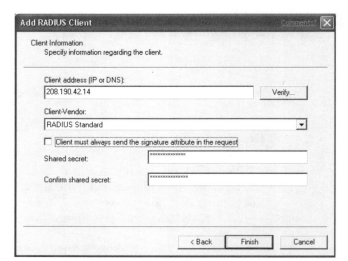

Figure 11.8
Add RADIUS Client.

Summary

VPNs take full advantage of the power of the Internet by creating secure, private networks contained within hostile, public networks. Windows .NET Server provides a completely operating system-integrated, end-to-end VPN solution. This chapter has covered the setup and installation of a Windows .NET Server VPN with attention to security issues. In addition, the suggested readings in the Appendix provide excellent resources for deploying your VPN solution.

Chapter 12

SECURITY CONFIGURATION TOOL SET

This chapter covers:

- The Security Configuration and Analysis snap-in
- The command-line tool Secedit.exe
- The Security Setting Extensions to Group Policy
- The Security Templates snap-in
- Using the Tool Set to configure security

Overview

Like its predecessor Windows 2000 Server, Windows .NET Server allows you to combine several administrative security tools into one powerful interface. This collection of utilities, known as the Security Configuration Tool Set, is comprised by the following functions:

1. Security Configuration and Analysis (SCA) snap-in
2. The command-line tool *Secedit.exe*
3. The Security Extensions to Group Policy
4. The Security Templates snap-in

The Security Configuration Tool Set allows you to organize many enterprise-wide configuration tasks into one powerful interface. The following sections show you how to use and configure these powerful tools. For convenience, many administrators will probably prefer to combine all of these tools into one MMC.

Security Configuration and Analysis Snap-in

The Security Configuration and Analysis (SCA) snap-in allows you to create and test various security configurations. The plain text files export as .inf files. Advanced users can work directly with the .inf files using a text editor. However, most users will prefer to work through the SCA snap-in GUI to prevent errors.

 Tip

The Security Configuration and Analysis snap-in works only on the local computer. You cannot use it to configure security across a domain or an organizational unit.

The SCA is useful for configuring security on the local system, but it cannot control policy across domains or organizational units. Nevertheless, it is useful for designing and testing security policies locally.

Creating the SCA Snap-in

To create the snap-in, type **MMC** at a console and click **Add** to add the SCA, the Security Templates, and the Group Policy, as shown in Figure 12.1.

Then you can save the MMC in a convenient location for later use. You now have a powerful diagnostic security tool set at your disposal.

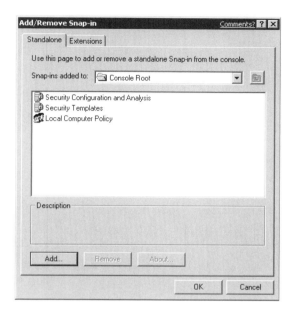

Figure 12.1
Add/Remove Snap-in.

Testing the Current Security Configuration

In order to test the current security configuration, you will first need to open a database. To do this, perform the following actions:

To Open an Existing Database

1. Right-click the **Security Configuration and Analysis** scope item.
2. Click **Open Database**.
3. Select a database, and then click **Open**.

To Create a New Database

1. Right-click the **Security Configuration and Analysis** scope item.
2. Click **Open Database**.
3. Type a new database name, and then click **Open**.
4. Select a security template to import, and then click **Open**.

Figure 12.2 shows how to open a sample database. In this case, we choose a database that we have previously created, arbitrarily named "cyrusdb1."

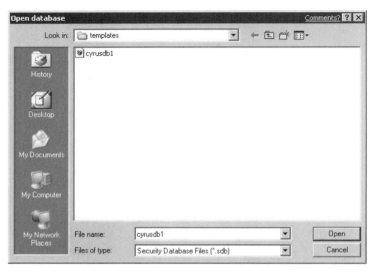

Figure 12.2
Security Configuration database.

If you have not created a database yet, or if you are creating a new one, you will automatically be presented with a dialog box asking you to choose from a list of sample templates. However, if you have opened an existing database, you will have to take an extra step to import a set of security configuration rules. To do this, simply right-click on the **Security Configuration and Analysis** branch. Figure 12.3 demonstrates this process.

Once you have selected **Import Template**, as shown in Figure 12.3, you must pick from a list of sample templates.

With time, you will develop a catalog of sample templates of your own. Some admins will have different templates for different situations, and will use these to test and to tweak security settings. For now, you can start by selecting **hisecdc**, as shown in Figure 12.4. The **hisecdc** template is a default configuration that comes with Windows .NET Server.

Table 12.1.   Security Areas

Area Name	Description
SECURITYPOLICY	Local policy and domain policy for the system, including account policies, audit policies, and so on
GROUP_MGMT	Restricted group settings for any groups specified in the security template
USER_RIGHTS	User logon rights and granting of privileges
REGKEYS	Security on local registry keys
FILESTORE	Security on local file storage
SERVICES	Security for all defined services

/log *logpath*	Path to the log file for the process. If not specified, the default is used.
/quiet	Suppresses screen and log output.

Export Security Settings

This command exports a stored template from a security database to a security template file.

```
secedit /export
```

Syntax

secedit /export [**/mergedPolicy**] [**/DB** *filename*] [**/CFG** *filename*] [**/areas** *area1 area 2...*] [**/log** *logPath*] [**/quiet**]

Parameters

/MergedPolicy	Merges and exports domain and local policy security settings.
/DB *filename*	Provides the path to a database that contains the template that will be exported. If a database is not provided, the system policy database is used.
/CFG *filename*	Path and name of a file where the template should be saved.
/areas *area1 area2...*	Specifies the security areas (See Table 12.2) to be exported to a template. The default is "all areas." Each area should be separated by a space.

225

Table 12.2. Security Areas to be Exported to a Template

Area Name	Description
SECURITYPOLICY	Local policy and domain policy for the system, including account policies, audit policies, and so on
GROUP_MGMT	Restricted group settings for any groups specified in the security template
USER_RIGHTS	User logon rights and granting of privileges
REGKEYS	Security on local registry keys
FILESTORE	Security on local file storage
SERVICES	Security for all defined services

/log *logpath*	Path to the log file for the process. If not specified, the default is used.
/quiet	Suppresses screen and log output.

Validate a Security Configuration File

This command validates the syntax of a security template you want to import into a database for analysis or application to a system.

```
secedit /validate
```

Syntax

secedit /validate *filename*

Parameters

filename   The file name of the security template you have created with Security Templates.

Security Setting Extensions to Group Policy

Once you have configured and tested local security policy using the Security Configuration and Analysis (SCA) snap-in, you can move on to configuring security across an entire domain or organizational unit. You can do this using the Security Setting Extensions to Group Policy editor.

The Security Settings Extension to the Group Policy Editor is used to define security configuration for groups of users or groups of computers within a Group Policy Object (GPO). The Security Settings extension can work automatically in the background to interpret a standard security configuration.

In order to get started in setting the wide area security policy, perform the following steps:

1. Go to **Start ➤ Settings ➤ Control Panel ➤ Administrative Tools**.
2. Open the **Active Directory Users and Computers** option.
3. Right-click on **Organizational Unit** and click **Properties**.
4. Click the **Group Policy** tab.
5. Select a **New** Group Policy.
6. Type a name for the new Group Policy Object.
7. Select the new Object and click **Edit**.
8. Expand **Computer Configuration ➤ Windows Settings ➤ Security Settings**.
9. Right-click on **Security Settings** and select **Import Policy**.
10. Click **Open** to adopt the new policy.

Security Templates Snap-in

The Security Templates snap-in provides a focal point for configuring and applying the entire system security configuration. As shown above, Windows .NET Server comes with a catalog of predefined security templates that cover a range of progressive security levels.

Security Templates can be used to configure the following areas:

- Account policies
- Local policies
- Event log
- Restricted groups
- System services
- Registry
- File system

Account Policies

A domain's account policy defines password settings, account lockout settings, and Kerberos settings. This is comprised of the Password Policy and the Account Lockout Policy. The Password Policy allows you to set the minimum and maximum password ages and lengths. The Account Lockout Policy lets you set the lockout time after failed login attempts. Domain accounts are configured at the domain, while local account policies are configured on the local computer.

Local Policies

Local policies cover auditing, user rights, and various other local options. In Windows .NET, "local" refers to any local machine, whether it is a domain controller or client computer. The local policies are comprised of the Audit Policy, User Rights Assignment, and Security Options.

The Audit Policy specifies what is recorded in the security log. User Rights Assignment controls local privileges. Finally, Security Options allow the administrator fine control over resources such as floppy drive access.

Event Log

The settings in Event Log allow you to control the configuration of the application, security, and system logs. Settings include maximum log sizes and guest access restrictions.

Restricted Groups

Restricted Groups allows you to have granular control over built-in groups with predefined capabilities. Default groups include Administrators, Power Users, Print Operators, and so on. You can also add your own custom groups with tailored privileges.

System Services

The System Services are configured for security in this list. This includes all services such as networking services, file and print services, and fax services.

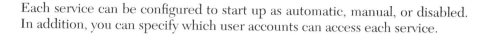

Each service can be configured to start up as automatic, manual, or disabled. In addition, you can specify which user accounts can access each service.

Registry

The Registry list contains the path and security descriptor of each key object. You can configure security on each individual registry key by right-clicking it here.

File System

You can use the File System list to set folder and file permissions. By loading a template into the security configuration and analysis tool, you can apply security settings to any file or folder.

Predefined Security Templates

Windows .NET Server provides a set of security templates for convenient out-of-the-box configuration and testing. By default, predefined security templates are stored in the following location:

Systemroot\Security\Templates

These predefined templates can be imported into a Group Policy object using the Security Settings tool or applied to local computer security using the Security Configuration and Analysis tool.

 Caution

Be sure to test the predefined security templates before applying them to your production network. Always test the templates first to ensure that you are not introducing weaknesses into your existing security configuration.

The predefined security templates that ship with Windows .NET Server are as follows (also see Figure 12.6):

- Setup security (setup security.inf) and Domain controller security (DC security.inf)

- Compatible workstation or server (compatws.inf)
- Secure workstation or server (securews.inf)
- Highly secure workstation or server (hisecws.inf)
- Secure domain controller (securedc.inf)
- Highly secure domain controller (hisecdc.inf)
- File system security (rootsec.inf)
- Removes the Terminal Server user SID from all system Access Control Lists (notssid.inf)

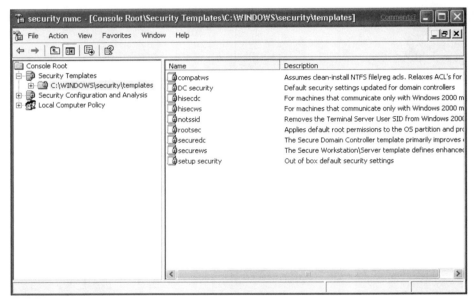

Figure 12.6
Predefined security templates.

Security Levels

The templates were designed to cover five common requirements for security:

- **Setup security.inf**

  After a clean install of Windows .NET Server, you are set at the baseline Setup security template by the default. **Setup security.inf** is different for each workstation or server.

Domain controllers use **setup security.inf** with the **DC security.inf** template. The DC security template defines system services settings that are specific for a domain controller.

- **Compatible (compat*.inf)**

  The default security configuration gives members of the local Users group strict security settings, while members of the local Power Users group have more liberal security settings. This default configuration enables certified applications to run for Users, while still allowing applications that are not certified to run for Power Users. If you need your users to run applications that are not certified, then you have the option of promoting your Users to Power Users. However, if Users are members of the Power Users group, this may compromise the security on your computer or network. Another option would be to assign users, by default, only as members of the Users group and then configure security so that applications not certified run successfully.

  The compatible template is designed for lowering the security levels on specific files, folders, and registry keys that are commonly accessed by applications. The compatible template allows most applications to run successfully under a User context. In addition, since it is assumed that the administrator applying the compatible template does not want users to be Power Users, all members of the Power Users group are removed.

- **Secure (secure*.inf)**

  The secure templates implement recommended security settings for all security areas except files, folders, and registry keys. These are not modified because file system and registry permissions are configured securely by default. The Secure template does remove all members of the Power Users group.

- **Highly secure (hisec*.inf)**

  The highly secure templates define security settings for network communications. The security areas are set to require maximum protection for network traffic and protocols used between computers in a .NET enterprise. As a result, such computers configured with a highly secure template can only communicate with other Windows 2000, Windows XP Pro, and Windows .NET Server machines. They will not be able to communicate with clients running Windows 95 or 98 or Windows NT.

- **System root security (rootsec.inf)**

  The **rootsec.inf** resets the default permission entries of the system root folder and propagates the permissions to all subfolders and files. In order to reset default permissions on all files and subfolders, you must use the setup **security.inf** template. The permission entries of the root folder are

231

inherited by all files and subfolders except anywhere a file or subfolder has explicit permissions set.

- **Removes the Terminal Server user SID from all system Access Control Lists (notssid.inf)**

  Applying this template will not increase security on your Terminal Server in any other way besides removing the Terminal Server User SID from all system Access Control lists. To enhance security you must enable Full Security mode for Terminal Server. Applying this template will not enable Full Security mode or affect the security mode in any way.

  Terminal Server can be enabled in one of two security modes: **Full Security,** which provides the most secure environment for your terminal server, and **Relaxed Security,** which allows access to the system registry, enabling most legacy applications to run as they did under Windows NT 4.0, Terminal Server Edition.

Summary

Windows .NET Server allows you to combine several administrative security tools into one interface. These tools include the Security Configuration and Analysis snap-in, the command-line tool secedit.exe, the Security Setting Extensions to Group Policy, and the Security Templates snap-in. This collection of powerful utilities is collectively known as the Security Configuration Tool Set.

Part V

Configuring Windows .NET Internet Security

Chapter 13

SECURING INTERNET
INFORMATION SERVER

This chapter covers:

- Overview of Internet Information Server
- Installing Internet Information Server
- Using the Microsoft Management Console
- Securing IIS WWW Server
- Securing IIS FTP Server
- Securing SMTP and NNTP services
- Explanation of known vulnerabilities

Overview

Although not part of the core security services in Windows .NET Server, because of popular demand for this information we have included a chapter on securing Microsoft's Internet Information Server (IIS). IIS is the single most hacked software application ever. Because of its high visibility, an enterprise Web site is a choice target for hackers with a political or egotistical agenda.

Caution

Do not ever install IIS on a machine that is also a domain controller; this can result in severe system compromise by hackers.

In Windows .NET, IIS has evolved into a robust Web server with a host of useful, built-in features. IIS can handle millions of Web site hits per day while at the same time serving dynamic and interactive media to your site visitors. Through its enhanced security and support of scripting languages such as ASP and PHP, IIS is growing in popularity.

Although the most popular Web server software is still Apache, Microsoft's IIS is rapidly growing in popularity and taking market share away from Apache. IIS not only provides worldwide Web services, but it also handles file transfer requests (FTP Server), mail requests (SMTP Server), and newsgroup requests (NNTP Server). In addition, because IIS is a Microsoft Corporation product, it comes with many extras such as data links, Visual Interdev support for large multidepartment programming projects, FrontPage support for live Web authoring, index services for quicker online searches, and much more. With Microsoft's big push for XML, .NET, and the global use of Passport authentication systems, IIS is destined for greatness.

Tip

Apache is a very secure, open-source UNIX alternative that also runs flaw-lessly on Windows platforms. If you would like to try an alternative to IIS, you can get the Apache server for free at www.apache.org.

Installation

The first step in setting up a secure IIS is to ensure that the system on which it is being installed is secure. This includes locking out all extra accounts, tightening down who has access to what, ensuring the hard drive is formatted with NTFS, and more. This chapter will review the security precautions that must be met before and during the secure installation of IIS.

Preinstall Checklist

Before installing IIS, the system must be configured securely and all extra components that could cause unauthorized access must be removed. The following lists the preventative measures you need to take and describes each one in detail.

Ensure that the hard drive is formatted using NTFS.

Windows .NET Server can be installed using FAT32 or NTFS file systems. While the FAT32 is thought to be the faster of the two, NTFS is much more secure. This is because NTFS allows the user to control every aspect of a system's security, all the way down to the file level. Using NTFS, an Administrator can set permissions on a file such as read only, no access, or full access. Using these permissions an Administrator can also log who tries to access what files and whether or not they were successful. This type of micromanagement may seem overly cautious, but it is the best way to repair a computer after it has been compromised is to use the details provided by the logging ability of NTFS.

Install the IIS behind closed doors and isolated from the Internet.

While this may seem paranoid, a hacker can scan a computer within 15 minutes or less of it being connected to the Internet for the first time. While IIS can be locked down fairly securely, during the time it takes to lock it down a hacker could have the time to install a Trojan, which would make any further attempts to secure the IIS meaningless.

In addition, another common belief among computer security experts is that the biggest threat to the security of a computer comes from inside the trusted domain, rather than from outside (i.e., the Internet). In high security environments, it is essential to build the IIS system within a controlled environment. Otherwise, the system could be compromised.

Install IIS in its own domain with no trusts.

When Windows .NET Server is installed, it should be in its own domain and have no other trusts with other domains. This prevents a hacker from relaying an attack farther into a network in case the computer running IIS is compromised.

Install IIS on a standalone server that is responsible for no other services.

Installing additional programs on an IIS (e.g., SQL Server or Exchange) will create more opportunities for a hacker to breach the security of the network. IIS has programming errors that lead to vulnerabilities, as do all programs. By adding programs to the server, a computer's chance of having a weakness grows exponentially. This is because many of these programs interact with each other and can escalate an individual, low-level security weakness into multiple, severe weaknesses.

Partition the hard drive so each service (e.g., WWW, FTP) is on its own volume.

By partitioning the hard drive so each service has its own volume or drive, a hacker can be stopped from using path traversing weaknesses that are a result of Unicode or other types of vulnerabilities. Simple commands such as "/.../" have been known to provide hackers with the ability to travel up the folder structure and give them access to sensitive files such as the *boot.ini* or script files. Using different drives stops the hacker at the root of the drive.

Ensure TCP/IP is the only protocol installed on the computer.

The Internet uses TCP/IP as its primary method of data transfer. Although there are situations where other protocols (e.g., IPX) may be necessary, adding these protocols increases the risk by adding complexity to the security policy.

Ensure IP routing is, and remains, disabled.

Microsoft has built a VPN solution into its operating system. However, this and other technologies require that the gateway device from the Internet to the internal network be able to pass data. Windows .NET Server has this ability, but it should be disabled if the computer is to be an IIS server. When enabled, the chance for a successful hack is greatly increased because a hacker can pass data into a network and internal computers can pass data directly out of a network.

Ensure file and print sharing for Microsoft networks is installed for NNTP or SMTP services.

If SMTP or NNTP will be installed, the Server service will be required. Thus, file and print sharing for Microsoft networks must be installed. If it is not, the Server service will not show up in the available services.

Unattended Installation

Once the requisite security measures have been met, it is time to install the IIS server. The best option for maintaining security is to use an unattended installation. This is because the *only* way to set up the FTPROOT and WWWROOT folders on different drives is to configure an Unattended Install file and allow the installation wizard to use it to set up and configure the IIS. Figure 13.1 illustrates an example of an Unattended Installation file that will install the IIS software on the C: drive, FTPROOT on E:, and WWWROOT on F:. As you can see, this installation file that was saved on the C: drive places

Figure 13.1
A sample Unattended Installation file.

the ROOT folders in an INETPUB directory. Although not a serious security risk, it is better to use a less obvious name.

Once the file has been created and put in an easily referenced location, start the install by following the subsequent instructions.

1. Click **Start ➤ Programs ➤ Accessories ➤ Command Prompt** to open a MS-DOS window.

2. Type **sysocmgr/I:%windir%\inf\sysoc.inf /u:*a:*\iis5.txt** replacing a:\iis5.txt with the drive, directory, and file name that you use to save the Unattended Install file, as shown in Figure 13.2.

Figure 13.2
C:\WINDOWS\System32\command.com.

3. After pressing **Enter**, you will see a series of windows (after a **Please wait** window, shown in Figure 13.3) informing you of the status of the installation.

Figure 13.3
Brief window before the installation wizard starts.

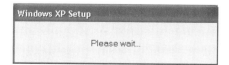

Tip

In order to install IIS, you will need to have a Windows CD-ROM or an image of the CD available to the destination computer.

4. As the IIS installer loads the program, you will see several screens, one of which is shown in Figure 13.4, describing the status of the installation.

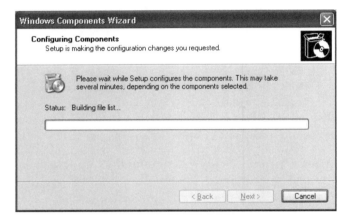

Figure 13.4
IIS Installation window.

Following is a list of many of the status messages you will see.

- Building file list…
- Examining installed files…
- Copying files…
- Installing Internet Information Services…

Once the installation is complete, the Windows Component Wizard window will close and you will be at the screen from which you originally started.

Post-Installation

Once the IIS has been successfully installed, the real work begins. At this point, the program is installed; however, there are many holes to seal and procedures that need to be accomplished to securely lock down the server installed.

User Accounts

The first thing that should be done is to remove the "Everyone" and "Guests" groups from the folders containing the IIS files. This is because IIS allows these groups full control of the publication directory (i.e., C:\Inetpub). These accounts, in combination with the knowledge that a typical installation places the Inetpub directory on the same drive as the key system files, can be used by hackers to gain unauthorized access to the files residing on the system.

To remove these dangerous groups, perform the following steps:

1. Find the **Inetpub** directory.
2. Right-click on the **Inetpub** folder and click **Properties.**
3. Click on the **Security** tab, shown in Figure 13.5.
4. Click on the group or user to delete and then click **Remove**.

The next user issue that needs attention is that of the IUSR_*computername* account. This default account is created during the installation of IIS. It is used by anonymous Web users to request information from the host computer. Therefore, this account needs special consideration and its privilege should be closely reviewed. In the case the IIS is to be used within a secure network only, it is recommended that the account be disabled. This would force all users to supply a valid user name and password before requesting information from the server.

Figure 13.5
Inetpub folder properties.

To adjust the privileges:

1. Click **Start ➤ Settings ➤ Control Panel ➤ Administrative Tools ➤ Computer Management ➤ Local Users and Groups ➤ Users** and right-click on the IUSR_*computername* account.
2. In the IUSR_*computername* Properties window, ensure that the **User cannot change password** option is checked as well as **Password never expires**.
3. If the IIS is to be used in a secure network only, also check **Account is disabled**. See Figure 13.6.
4. Click **OK** to save the changes.
5. Next click **Local Users and Groups ➤ Users** and double-click the **Guests** group.
6. Highlight the IUSR_*computername* account and click **Remove**. See Figure 13.7.

In addition to these rights, the account should only be listed as a local account, not a domain-wide account, and it must have the right to log on locally. These settings are set up upon installation and should not need adjustment. However, you should remove the right to **Access this computer from the network** and the **Log on as a batch job** rights that are enabled.

Figure 13.6
IUSR_*computername* Properties window.

Figure 13.7
Removing IUSR_*computername* from Guest accounts.

To change account rights:

1. Click **Start ➤ Settings ➤ Control Panel ➤ Administrative Tools ➤ Local Security Policy ➤ Local Policies.**
2. Double-click on the right to be adjusted.
3. Click on the IUSR_*computername* account and click **Remove**. See Figure 13.8.
4. Click **OK** or **Apply** to save the changes.

Once the existing accounts have been altered or removed to maximize security, it is recommended that you create two new groups: IISUsers and IISAdmins. Once created, they can be populated with individual accounts. By controlling permissions and rights at the group level, it becomes easier to monitor and adjust who has rights to what resources. If the server is to host several client sites, you should create an IISAdmins group for each site and use the IISUsers account to hold the IUSR_*computername* account and any other accounts that are to be used exclusively for Web read-only access. These groups can then be used to assign individual accounts with separate rights.

Once these groups are created add the IUSR_*computername* account to the IISUsers group and any administrative accounts to the IISAdmin account. These groups will be used to control the NTFS permissions that are set on each file and folder on a hard drive formatted with the NTFS.

Figure 13.8
Removing the **Access this computer from the network** right for the IUSR_*computername* account.

Services

During the installation of both Windows and IIS, numerous services are also installed that are not needed by the OS or any of the software used on the computer. Services are actually small programs that run in the background. They usually run at a low level and communicate directly with the hardware layer. Similar to daemons that run in the °nix environment, services not only use up memory, they also increase the chance that a computer becomes vulnerable to a hacker attack. Table 13.1 lists the services that are not needed by a standalone Web server. Note that some of the services are required if the computer is to participate in a network.

Table 13.1.   Services Not Needed by a Standalone Web Server

Service Name	Additional Notes
Alerter	
ClipBook Server	
Computer Browser	
DHCP Client	
Distributed File System	

Table 13.1. Services Not Needed by a Standalone Web Server (Continued)

Service Name	Additional Notes
Distributed Link Tracking Systems Client	
Distributed Link Tracking Systems Client	
FTP Publishing Service	Disabled unless user's require FTP services
IPSEC policy agent Disabled unless IPSEC policies will be used	
Licensing Logging Service	
Logical Disk Manager Administrator Service	
Messenger	
Net Logon	Disabled unless domain users are required to log on to the server, this service is required to communicate with the domain controller
Network DDE	
Network DDE DSDM	
Print Spooler	
Remote Registry Service	
Removable Storage	
RPC Locator	Required if user is doing remote administration
RunAS Service	
Server Service	Must be started if server will run the SMTP or NNTP service of IIS, for administration purposes
Task Scheduler	
TCP/IP NetBIOS Helper	
Telephony	
Windows Installer	

Once the service is installed, it is configured to run in one of three ways:

- **Automatic**: Used when the service needs to be started during the OS boot or when a program is initialized.
- **Manual:** Used when the service is not needed during typical day-to-day operations, but may be started with the execution of another program.
- **Disable:** The service is turned off and configured to remain so even as an execution is attempted.

To uninstall or disable a service:

1. Click **Start ➤ Settings ➤ Control Panel ➤ Administrative Tools ➤ Services** (Figures 13.9–13.11).
2. Right-click on the service to be adjusted.
3. Select **Stop** to temporarily turn off the service (*Note*: The service will return to its default status as configured in Properties upon computer reboot).
4. Select **Properties** to permanently adjust the service configuration.
5. Under the **Startup** type menu, select the desired option.

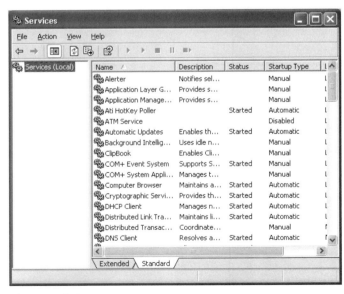

Figure 13.9
Windows .NET Server Services window.

Figure 13.10
FTP Publishing Services Properties window.

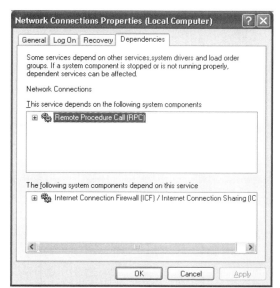

Figure 13.11
Network Connections Services Properties window.

Caution

Before disabling or stopping any service, check its dependencies to ensure that it is not required by any other services. If it is, the other services will not work properly. For example, the Internet Connection Firewall service requires the Network Connection service to run.

Securing the Metabase

One of the more commonly overlooked security risks involved with the operation of IIS is that of securing the metabase file. The metabase file is used by IIS in the same aspect as the registry is used by the operating system. It holds properties and settings that are used by IIS to control its operation.

The advantage of using the metabase file is threefold. For example, since the metabase file is exclusively used by IIS, its information can be accessed faster. In addition, because IIS is the only program that needs access to this file, the data in the metabase file can be made secure through encryption. The final advantage is that the metabase file can hold more detailed information than its counterpart, the registry.

While the data in the metabase file is safe from intruders, the file itself is not. In other words, if a hacker were to replace the original metabase file with a file of his or her own making, the hacker could shut down the IIS or compromise it by using another, less secure configuration.

In the case of the metabase file, the best security is obscurity. In other words, the file should be moved from its default location, \Winnt\system32\inetsrv, to another, less obvious location. The only change that needs to be made to the system to allow this action is to add a new key to the registry. To do this, follow the subsequent instructions.

Caution

The registry is a very sensitive part of the operating system. DO NOT make changes without knowing and understanding the outcome of these changes. In addition, you should ALWAYS make a backup of your registry the moment you open it, in case of a power loss or unrecoverable error.

1. Turn off the IIS services.
2. Move and/or rename the metabase.bin file.
3. Click on **Start ➤ Run**, type **regedit**, and hit **OK**.
4. Click **File ➤ Export** and save a copy of the registry to a safe location.

Caution

> *Ensure the backup registry file is stored in a location not normally accessed by the computer's users. If the registry backup is inadvertently double-clicked, its contents will overwrite any changes made in the registry since the date the backup file was created.*

5. Locate the key named **HKEY_LOCAL_MACHINE\SOFTWARE \Microsoft\InetMgr\Parameters**.
6. With **Parameters** highlighted, click **Edit ➤ New ➤ String** value (Figure 13.12).

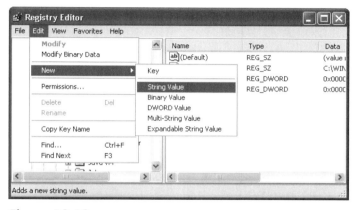

Figure 13.12
Creating a new registry key.

7. When the New Value key appears, name it **Metadata File.**
8. Double-click the **Metadata File** and enter the new location and name of the metabase.bin file, including the full path and file name.
9. Close the registry.

This registry entry tells IIS where the configuration file is located when it starts up. Although this procedure will secure the file, it does assume that the registry is secure. If a hacker can gain access to the data stored in the registry through the unauthorized use of an Administrator or System account, the file can still be compromised.

Backing Up/Restoring the Metabase

In addition to securing the Metabase, it is important to make regular backups in case the system falls prey to an attack, or simply crashes. There are three ways that the Metabase.bin file can be saved, which include the following:

- **Secure**: The secure method uses the IIS snap-in to perform a backup of the metabase.bin file, which is then encrypted with a password. Only those with the correct password will have access to the data in the file.
- **Insecure**: This method uses the IIS snap-in to perform a regular backup of the metabase.bin file. Anyone can restore the data in this file to an existing IIS installation.
- **Legacy**: This method uses third-party programs or a simple batch file to copy and replace the metabase.bin file.

The following describes how to perform a secure and insecure backup. If you wish to use a legacy program, consult that program documentation.

Secure Backup

1. Open the Internet Services Manager by selecting **Start ➤ Control Panel ➤ Administrative Tools ➤ Internet Information Services**.
2. Select the computer to back up.
3. Click **Action ➤ All Tasks ➤ Backup/Restore Configuration**, shown in Figure 13.13.

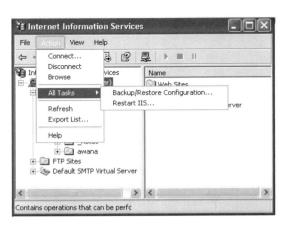

Figure 13.13
Backup/Restore Configuration menu selection.

4. Click **Create backup**. See Figure 13.14.

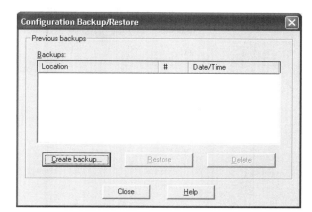

Figure 13.14
IIS Configuration Backup/Restore
window.

5. Enter backup name, check **Encrypt backup using password**, and enter a strong password. See Figure 13.15.

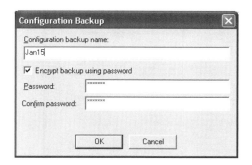

Figure 13.15
Configuration Backup window.

Insecure Backup

1. Open the Internet Services Manager by selecting **Start ➤ Control Panel ➤ Administrative Tools ➤ Internet Information Services**.
2. Select the computer to back up.
3. Click **Action ➤ All Tasks ➤ Backup/Restore Configuration.**
4. Click **Create backup**.
5. Enter backup name and select **OK**.

Restore from Backup

Inevitably, you will need to restore the settings. This is a relatively simple task, but can take some time and will require the restarting of IIS.

To restore the metabase.bin settings:

1. Open the Internet Services Manager by selecting **Start ➤ Control Panel ➤ Administrative Tools ➤ Internet Information Services**.
2. Select the computer to back up.
3. Click **Action ➤ All Tasks ➤ Backup/Restore Configuration**.
4. Click **Restore**.
5. If required, enter password.

Using NTFS to Secure File Access

Once the accounts have been set up and the metabase.bin file made secure, the next step is to set up the NTFS permissions on the existing folders and files that were installed with the IIS.

This is a complicated process and takes a solid understanding of how IIS and Web users call upon and process files on the Web server. Table 13.2 provides us with an excellent map to securing the files used by IIS 5 or 6.

Table 13.2. Securing Files Used by IIS 5 or 6

Type of Data	Example Directories	Data Examples	NTFS File Permissions	IIS 5.0 Permissions
Static Content	\Inetpub\wwwroot\Images \Inetpub\wwwroot\home \Inetpub\ftproot\ftpfiles	HTML, Images, FTP downloads, etc.	Administrators (Full Control) System (Full Control) WebAdmins (Read & Execute, Write, Modify) Authenticated User (Read & Execute) Anonymous (Read & Execute)	Read
FTP Uploads (if required)	\Inetpub\ftproot\dropbox	Directory used as a place for users to store documents for review prior to the Admin making them available to everyone	Administrators (Full Control) WebAdmins or FTPAdmins (Read & Execute, Write, Modify) Specified Users (Write)	Write

Table 13.2. Securing Files Used by IIS 5 or 6 (Continued)

Type of Data	Example Directories	Data Examples	NTFS File Permissions	IIS 5.0 Permissions
Script Files	\Inetpub\wwwroot\scripts	.ASP	Administrators (Full Control) System (Full Control) WebAdmins (Read & Execute, Write, Modify) Anonymous: special access (Execute)	Scripts only
Other Executable and Include Files	\WebScripts\executables \WebScripts\Include	.exe, .dll, .cmd, .pl, .lnc, .shtml, .shtm	Administrators (Full Control) System (Full Control) WebAdmins (Read & Execute, Write, Modify) Authenticated Users: special access (Execute) Anonymous: special access (Execute)	Scripts only or Scripts and Executables (Depending on necessity)
Metabase	\WINNT\system32\Inetsrv	MetaBase.bin	Administrators (Full Control) System (Full Control)	N/A

Once the user accounts and permissions for those accounts, services, and folder properties have been secured, it is time to move on to the IIS and its associated settings. The next few segments of this chapter describe in detail how to secure IIS Web and FTP servers.

Using the Internet Service Manager (ISM)

The ISM is actually an extension of the Microsoft Management Console (MMC). The MMC is simply a standard console used to control various services and programs. By standardizing the way programs are supervised, Windows .NET Server administrators can more effectively control their systems. To access the

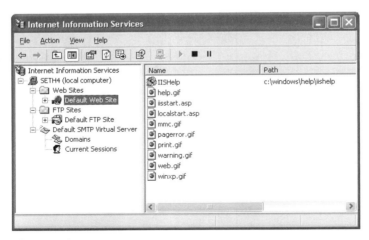

Figure 13.16
Internet Information Services

ISM click on **Start** ➤ **Control Panel** ➤ **Administrative Tools** ➤ **Internet Information Services**.

As illustrated in Figure 13.16, we have installed the WWW service and the FTP service. Each of these services is represented by a main folder under the IIS server (SETH4). By navigating the ISM tree, you can access the global properties of a service or the individual properties of each Web site or FTP site that the IIS contains.

WWW Service

The WWW service is the most commonly installed component of IIS. This service accepts incoming requests from the Internet or local network, processes the request, and sends the respective Web pages back to the client. This includes processing any programming, database connections, encryption, or any other service required by its clients.

Because the client computer accesses resources on the IIS, there are numerous security issues that need to be addressed to ensure a client is properly restricted from system files, password files, and other important data that should not be passed via the WWW service.

The first step in securing the WWW server is to configure the global settings upon which the rest of the WWW configurations are based. To do this, right-click on the **Web Site** folder and select **Properties**. This will open a screen similar to Figure 13.17.

Figure 13.17
Web Sites Properties.

Master Web Site Properties

The WWW service is configured in several layers. At the top is the Master Web Site properties that are inherited by any specific sites. Using a setup like this, an Administrator can ensure that any newly created Web site is secure. The following describes each of the tabs and their sections as they apply to security.

ISAPI Filters

This is the first property sheet visible upon opening the Master Web Site properties. While the settings on this tab are not direct security concerns, knowing the purpose of this sheet is important. Each of the filters listed represents a .dll file that gives functionality to the Web server. In the case that a vulnerability is discovered that exploits one of these files, you will need to use this page to remove or change the settings for the Web server. These files can only be installed and adjusted from this window.

Home Directory

The next tab in the properties window is Home Directory. This window, as seen in Figure 13.18, is used to control the global default settings for each

Figure 13.18
Web Sites Properties.

Web site under its control. We recommend that you enable **Log visits** and leave the rest of the options unchecked. The following discusses each of the options in detail and our suggested setting for them.

Permissions

Read (Disabled): While a Web site will need to be configured as Read to allow users to view any resources, we suggest that each site be manually configured to allow read access after the site is created. This will ensure no access is granted until the site is ready for clients.

Write (Disable): This option should always be disabled, unless you want to give users the ability to write to all Web sites. This setting can be enabled, if required, at the site level.

Directory Browsing (Disable): This option should always be disabled. By allowing this, you give users the ability to view all the file names and folders in a Web site. This only serves to provide hackers with more information they can exploit.

Logging (Enable): This will enable logging on each Web site you add later. While not necessary for operation, it is best to maintain vigorous logging in case a hack attempt occurs.

Index this Resource (Disable): This option should remain disabled at the global level. If searching ability is requested by individual Web sites, it can be enabled at the local level.

Execute Permissions (None): This will ensure that no users can run script files or programs by default. If individual sites require this, it can be enabled at the local level.

Application Settings

By default this section is correctly set up, with the exception of the sheets settings available by clicking on the **Configuration** button. The **Application name:** should remain blank and **Execute Permissions:** should be kept at **None**.

 Tip

Unmap any unnecessary file extensions. This will limit the risk of the Web server falling victim to new vulnerabilities.

Application Configuration: This set of property sheets controls the internals of the Web server. It is important to understand how the Web server will respond to requests. Every time a client requests an ASP page from IIS, it must first process the file using a program. The application configuration is responsible for controlling this. In addition, the IIS server must be configured for debugging, timeouts, and more. If the server is configured properly at the Master level, the lower levels will inherit the settings.

- *Mappings*: This sheet, shown in Figure 13.19, is used to link all file extensions to the files responsible for their processing. It is recommended that you remove any extensions you will not want the Web sites to incorporate into their services. (e.g., .htr files are used to perform remote password administration).
- *Options*: The Options sheet, shown in Figure 13.20, is used to set the timeout settings for both the session and the script. The default settings are adequate. However, if you are experiencing a DoS (Denial of Service) attack, you may want to decrease the timeout settings. What could be a simple programming error on a Web page can be misinterpreted as a DoS attack. These settings need to be a balance between programming needs and security threats.
  In addition to timeout settings, ensure the **Enable parent paths** is disabled. If enabled, a hacker could exploit folder traversing vulnerabilities.

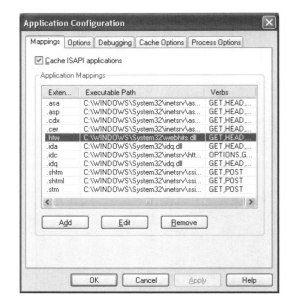

Figure 13.19
WWW Master Site Application
Configuration—Mappings sheet.

Figure 13.20
WWW Master Site Application
Configuration—Options sheet.

   Caution

> *Be careful in limiting the default timeout settings. If an ASP script exceeds the timeout, it will return as "failed." This could prevent an application from operating properly.*

Debugging: This sheet, shown in Figure 13.21, defines the debugging options for the WWW server. While useful in development machines, sending detailed ASP errors back to the requesting client could reveal sensitive information. In situations of high security, it is recommended that a generic message is sent instructing the user to contact the Webmaster.

Figure 13.21
WWW Master Site Application
Configuration—Debugging sheet.

Cache Options: This sheet, shown in Figure 13.22, controls the speed in which ASP scripts are processed by the IIS. If the results of the ASP script can be stored, the next time the script is called it will not have to be processed.

Process Options: This sheet, shown in Figure 13.23, is set up correctly by default. It holds two important settings that should be left as is. The **Write unsuccessful client requests to event log** should be enabled because it will capture a hacker performing a brute force or scan attack on a server. Finally, the CGI script timeout follows the same suggested guidelines as the ASP script timeout configured in the Options sheet.

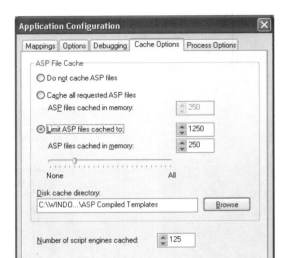

Figure 13.22
WWW Master Site—Application
Configuration Cache Options sheet.

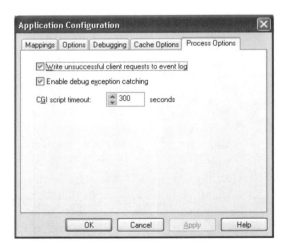

Figure 13.23
WWW Master Site—Application
Configuration Process Option sheet.

Directory Security

The other important properties sheet of the WWW Master Site, with respect to security, is the Directory Security tab (see Figure 13.24). This tab is used to control the access level and authentication methods for all users who request information from the Web site.

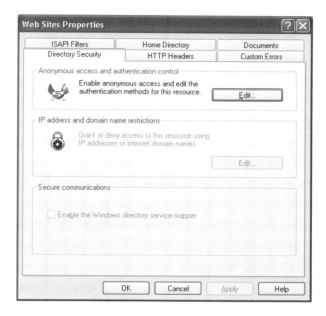

Figure 13.24
WWW Master Site Properties—
Directory Security sheet.

Anonymous Access and Authentication Control. This section is used to configure the accounts that are used to access the IIS server resources. To adjust the settings, click the **Edit** button.

The Authentication Method the Web site(s) use to control user access is mainly determined by whether the site is on the Internet or an Intranet. If the Web site is to be used solely by users on a Windows-based Intranet, a domain controller should control their access. Therefore, **Anonymous Access** should be unchecked. This allows greater access control, as individual accounts can be granted access to Web server resources. However, if the Web server is primarily to be used for sites that will be accessed via the Internet, it is recommended that **Anonymous Access** remain checked.

Although not typically required, you can change the account used to control anonymous access to the server. Using the **Browse** button, you can select another account through which access is allowed. You can also uncheck the **Allow IIS to control password** option and enter your own password.

Changing the Anonymous account is often done because the IUSR_*computername* resets the **Log on as batch job** and **Access this computer from the network** rights each time the computer is rebooted or the IIS server is restarted.

The final setting that can be adjusted, depending on your needs, is the **Authenticated access** setting. More information on authentication methods follows this section.

261

Authentication Overview

Digest Authentication for Windows Domain Servers

This is used only if the Web server is operating on a Windows 2000 Server or .NET Server and the passwords must be stored in a file on the local server. However, this adds an extra complication to the Web server configuration and is not completely secure.

While similar in features to Basic authentication, Digest authentication uses a more secure means of passing credentials. For a client to gain access, the following must occur:

1. Server passes some data to client.
2. Client combines server information with username, password, and some extra data to create a hash.
3. Hash is sent to server with client's data and it too creates a hash.
4. If the hash matches, the client is granted access.

When this option is selected, it is important to note that the Administrator must have a password policy in effect and evoked. Without this requirement met, Digest authentication will not work.

There are also weaknesses with the Digest Authentication RFC that make it vulnerable to several types of attack. However, if the only other option is Basic Authentication, Digest should be used. Microsoft cannot patch the weaknesses, as they are design errors that were in place before Microsoft adopted it. Any changes by Microsoft would make Digest noncompliant with RFC standards.

Basic Authentication

This authentication method sends passwords in clear text. While it does provide a measure of protection, a rogue sniffer on the network could capture the passwords and provide a hacker with an easy target.

If this authentication option is your only choice, it should be used in conjunction with SSL. To use SSL, you must obtain a Server Certificate, require a specific port to use for data transfer, and disable all other forms of authentication.

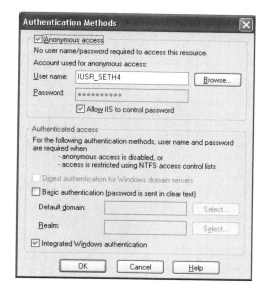

Figure 13.25
WWW Master Site Properties—
Directory Security—Authentication
Methods sheet.

Integrated Windows Authentication (Figure 13.25)

This option is the best for any time anonymous access is disabled or access is restricted using NTFS access control lists. It uses Windows NT Challenge/ Response and Kerberos v5 protocol. However, in order to use this type of authentication the client must be using Internet Explorer.

One or all of these types of authentication can be used. The client will first try Anonymous authentication, and if that fails the server will send a list of all the accepted types of authentication. The client will try each acceptable type until the list is complete or access is granted.

Default Web Site Properties

If the Master Web Sites Properties were configured according to the previous instructions, every individual Web site should be locked down by default. This ensures that you control who has access to what and removes the threat that an important setting is forgotten. With the exception of ISAPI Filters and Web Site, the property sheets are similar at the Site/folder/file level; therefore, you can use the following recommendations throughout.

To access each site's individual properties, right-click on the root folder of the Web site (e.g., Default Web Site) and select **Properties.** This will open a window similar to Figure 13.26.

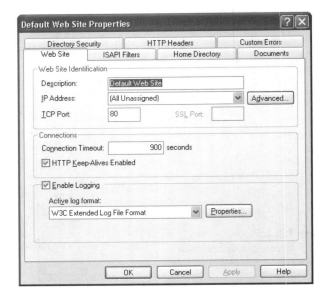

Figure 13.26
Default Web Site Properties.

Web Site

The first properties sheet you will see is labeled Web Site. This sheet controls various settings that are important to configure properly in order to keep a site secure. The following will describe each part and its security implications.

Web Site Identification (Figures 13.27, 13.28)

Description: This is the name that will be used in the ISM tree to identify the Web site.

IP address: This is the IP address through which the Web site will be accessed. If the server hosts several sites for several networks, and one site needs to be accessed explicitly from one network, the IP address for that network can be selected. This allows access only on the selected NIC.

TCP/SSL port: This allows you to configure a Web site to run on a custom port. This provides a small measure of protection if the Web site needs to be hidden from casual surfers, or if there are multiple Web sites operating through one NIC.

Advanced: This allows you to configure a site's specific access options. If the Web hosts more than one site, the Advanced options allow the administrator to use either the Host Name Header or the IP address to control access to additional sites. This allows more than one site to run on one NIC with one IP address.

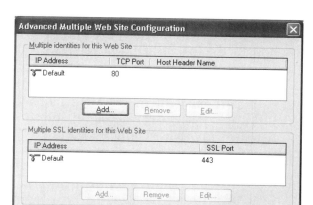

Figure 13.27
Use the Advanced Multiple Web Site Configuration sheet for adding virtual hosts.

Figure 13.28
Enter Host Header Name, port, and IP address to define a virtual host.

Connections

Connection timeout: This setting controls how long a client's session will remain open if there is no activity. Keep this setting at or under 900 to reduce the chance of an inadvertent Denial of Service (DoS) condition, which could occur if several connections were established at one time and then left inactive. Due to the limited number of open connections, an abundance of inactive sessions will cause a server to stop responding.

HTTP keep-alives: HTTP keep-alives are used to keep a session active across several requests. This keeps the number of sessions per client at a minimum and reduces the threat of an inadvertent DoS condition.

Enable Logging

Logging should always be enabled. In case of an attack, the logs will help you patch holes quickly.

Active log format: This setting should always be kept on its default setting, "W3C Extended Log File Format." This type of logging allows for more customization of the items recorded.

Properties:

- The **General Properties** sheet allows you to configure various options. Typically, you should keep the default settings, with the exception of the log file location. By changing the log file location, you provide an extra layer of protection in case the server is hacked. Any good hacker will remove all trace of himself or herself; thus, making the log files difficult to locate will also help to keep them intact.
- The **Extended Properties** sheet allows you to adjust what information you want logged. If you suspect a hacker or need to troubleshoot an error, enabling more options may provide the missing piece of information you need (Figures 13.29, 13.30).

Figure 13.29
Extended Logging Properties sheet.

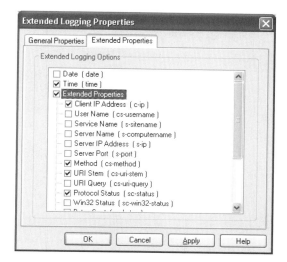

Figure 13.30
Extended Logging Properties sheet.

Home Directory

The Home Directory is the second of four key sheets that will need adjusting. This sheet controls the general access permissions for the Web site, where the Web site is physically located, and more. The following will review the purpose and recommended settings for each area on this sheet.

When connecting to this resource, the content should come from. This part of the sheet directs incoming requests to the physical location. This can be used to send a user's request to a different drive, a different computer on the network, or even to another URL. While space limitations may require this setting to be adjusted, all resources are typically located on the same computer running the server software.

Local Path. This is the physical path to the resources being served to connecting clients. Previously, we discussed that resources should be stored at a location other than the root drive of the host computer. If this is not the case, you can select a location using the **Browse** button.

In addition to the path, this area of the sheet is used to control the general permissions given to the Web site. The only options that should be checked are that of **Read** and **Log Visits**. Providing any more permission at this level can inadvertently cause a misconfigured folder that could be used by a hacker to gain unauthorized access to the computer. Control the other access levels at the folder or file level, not the Web site level.

Application settings. These settings are used to configure the permissions needed for scripts, executables, and dll files. There are several very important considerations to be made regarding these settings.

Execute Permissions: This setting tells the server how to interpret scripts and executables located on the site or individual folder.

- **None**—If there are no scripts located in the Web site, this is the preferred selection. With this set, any executable or script file will be simply read as it is written.
- **Scripts only**—This is used if the Web site requires scripting to access databases or process information. This setting should only be set if the *Read* permissions are disabled. This is to prevent a client from reading the source code in the script file and gleaning user names and/or passwords that may exist.
- **Scripts and Executables**—Allows any executable, dll, or script to be run. This should only be used in the case that the Web server or clients require the support of an executable file. Ensure the folder does not have NTFS Write permissions set or else a hacker could upload a file to the server and execute it remotely.

Application Protection: This option should always be set at medium or high. Using medium will prevent IIS applications from interfering with each other, and using high will cause all applications to run in their own memory space. This will avoid crashing and buffer overflow problems.

 Tip

Server-side includes (SSI) and Internet Database Connector applications cannot be run in a separate memory space from the Web server's memory space.

Application Configuration: By clicking this button, you can access the details of the Web applications settings. Adjusting these options properly can help to secure a Web server. Upon opening this sheet, you will be able to adjust application mappings, debugging options, and execution options (Figure 13.31).

- **Mappings**—This sheet, shown in Figure 13.32, is used to control the actions a Web server takes when a file is executed. When a resource is called upon, its extension is compared to the Mappings list to determine if a .dll or .exe file is used to process the information. The Mappings are important to monitor and control to reduce the risk of a hacker exploiting a new or known vulnerability.

Figure 13.31
Default Web Site Properties—Home Directory sheet.

Figure 13.32
Default WWW Site Properties—Home Directory—Application Configuration—Mappings sheet.

• **Options**—This sheet, shown Figure 13.33, has two important settings. The first is the **Session timeout** length. This option is used to control how long a user has access to Web site resources after the first

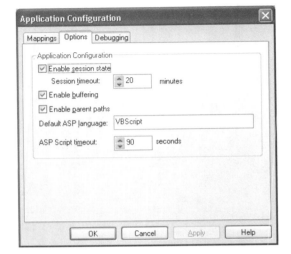

Figure 13.33
Default WWW Site Properties—
Home Directory—Application
Configuration—Options sheet.

request. By reducing this time, a user is forced to revalidate herself. Although reducing this time can increase security in case a session is hijacked, it can also annoy users if the session time is set too low.

The second option that should be adjusted is that of **Enable parent paths**. This option should be disabled to prevent a hacker from traveling up or down a folder and accessing a folder with permissions that could allow a hacker to write or execute a file.

- **Debugging**—This sheet, shown in Figure 13.34, is used to configure settings related to how the Web server reacts to an error. The only

Figure 13.34
Default WWW Site Properties—
Home Directory—Application
Configuration—Debugging sheet.

setting that should be adjusted on this page is **Send detailed ASP error messages to client**. If this is not required, it is best to disable this option. ASP error messages can reveal information useful to a hacker, such as full file paths. If there are no ASP applications under development, or being debugged, this option can be disabled.

Documents. The Documents properties sheet, shown in Figure 13.35, is important to security for one reason: the **Enable Default Document** option. This option should be checked to force any client computer to view one of the listed files. If this is not checked, a client could view the directory structure of the Web site or folder they are requesting. This could give a client information about file names, which could be exploited by other attacks.

Figure 13.35
Default WWW Site Properties—
Documents sheet.

Directory Security. This tab, shown in Figure 13.36, is available at the master site, Web site, directory, virtual directory, and file level. The security properties are relatively the same at each level, and can be adjusted to meet the requirements.

The property sheet is split up into three main sections. Each section is important to security and will be discussed in detail.

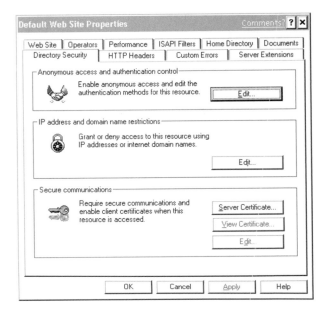

Figure 13.36
Directory Security Properties screen.

Anonymous access and authentication control. The Authentication Methods the Web site uses to control user access is mainly determined by whether the site is on the Internet or an Intranet. If the Web site is to be used solely by users on a Windows-based Intranet, a domain controller should control their access. Therefore, **Anonymous Access** should be unchecked. This allows greater access control, as individual accounts can be granted access to Web server resources. However, if the Web server is primarily to be used for sites that will be accessed via the Internet, it is recommended that **Anonymous Access** remain checked (Figure 13.37).

Although not typically required, you can change the account used to control anonymous access to the server. Using the **Browse** button, you can select another account through which access is allowed. You can also uncheck the **Allow IIS to control password** option and enter your own password.

Changing the Anonymous account is often done because the IUSR_*computername* resets the **Log on as batch job** and **Access this computer from the network** rights each time the computer is rebooted or the IIS is restarted.

The final setting that can be adjusted depending on your needs is the **Authenticated access** setting. More information on authentication methods can be found under the Master WWW Properties section.

Figure 13.37
Default WWW Site Properties—
Directory Security—Authentication
Methods sheet.

IP Address and Domain Name Restrictions (Figures 13.38, 13.39). This option is used to designate who can (or cannot) access the Web site as defined by the client's IP address and/or host name. By selecting **Granted Access** or **Denied Access,** the list will either allow or prohibit incoming requests. **Granted Access** allows access ONLY to those listed, while **Denied Access** restricts access to those listed. Of the two, **Granted Access** provides the greatest level of security, but it is so restrictive that it can only be used within a local network or in very specific cases.

There are several options available that can be used to filter the incoming requests. They are:

- *Single computer:* This option uses a list of specific IP addresses.
- *Group of computers:* This option uses a network ID and subnet mask as its filter.
- *Domain name:* This verifies the client's IP address against a list of accepted domain names. This option will degrade the performance, as each connection must be verified by a DNS reverse lookup.

Secure Communications. This option is used to configure the settings used when a Secure Socket Layer connection is made between the client and the host. Using secure certificates, an encrypted connection can be established between a client and host, thus ensuring that sensitive data (e.g., credit card numbers) is not captured by a network sniffer.

Figure 13.38
IP Address and Domain Name
Restrictions.

Figure 13.39
Deny Access On.

IIS supports the use of Server Certificates to ensure that data transferred between it and clients on the Internet remains secure. The following instructions will describe how to set up and enable SSL on your computer.

1. Under the **Directory Security** tab, click **Server Certificate**.
2. Click **Next** at the Welcome screen.
3. Select **Create a new certificate** option, shown in Figure 13.40.

Figure 13.40
IIS Server Certificate select window.

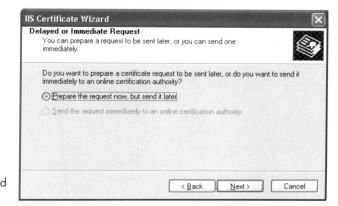

Figure 13.41
IIS Certificate Wizard request method window.

4. Select **Prepare the request now, but send it later**, shown in Figure 13.41.

You can select the other option if available. This will automate the sending of the output file to your selection of certificate vendors, as long as it is on the list provided by the IIS Certificate Wizard.

5. Enter a name for the certificate.

This name should be easy to remember. While a small business may only use one certificate, ISPs have hundreds of certificates they have to manage. It is important for the name to convey its intent (See Figure 13.42).

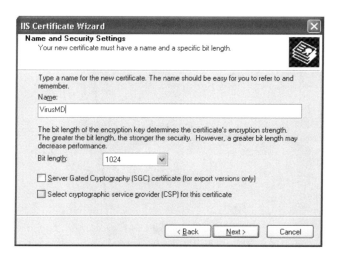

Figure 13.42
IIS Certificate Wizard name settings window.

6. Select a bit length option for the certificate.

Caution

Before selecting an option, ensure the vendor will support the level of encryption required. In addition, the longer the bit length, the longer data transmission will take. Only select the amount of encryption that is required.

7. If required, check the Server Gated Cryptology (SGC) or Cryptographic Service Provider (CSP) options.

SGC: Commonly used in banking environments, SGC is a Microsoft encryption solution that provides an additional type of security for online data transfer.

CSP: When a certificate is created it is passed to a program stored on the computer called the CSP. The CSP then creates either a private/public key pair used in software authentication, or it instructs any hardware authentication devices (such as a Smart Card) to create the private/public key pair.

8. Enter the organization name and department to which the SSL certificate will belong, as shown in Figure 13.43.

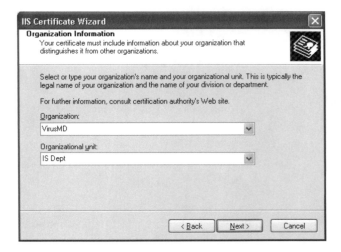

Figure 13.43
IIS Certificate Wizard organization information window.

 Tip

The information entered as part of the SSL certificate setup will be verified by a certificate authority (i.e., VeriSign).

276

9. Enter the domain name of the Web site to use the certificate.

 Caution

> *You must enter the exact name of the Web address to be protected. Otherwise any visitor who wants to use SSL will see that the certificate does not match the Web site for which it was created.*

10. Enter a common name (i.e., domain name), as shown in Figure 13.44.

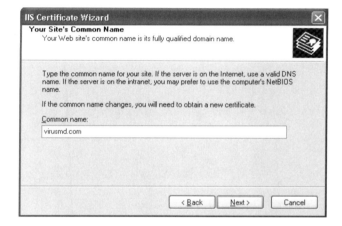

Figure 13.44
IIS Certificate Wizard domain name window.

11. Enter the country, state, and city of the company headquarters to which the SSL certificate will be provided. See Figure 13.45.

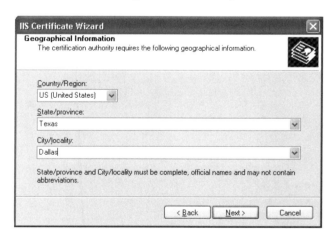

Figure 13.45
IIS Certificate Wizard geographical information window.

Caution

Ensure that you enter the entire state name. Abbreviations are not allowed.

12. Enter the location where the certificate request file is to be saved. This should be local and secure. See Figure 13.46.

Figure 13.46
IIS Certificate Wizard file output window.

13. Click **Next** and **Finish** to finalize the creation of the certificate.

At this time the certificate request has been generated. Send the file to a certificate authority (i.e., Verisign.com), which will validate the information and provide you with a secure certificate to use for the Web server. To install the certificate, simply click **Server Certificate** again and select **Process the pending request and install the certificate,** shown in Figure 13.47. This will complete the SSL install.

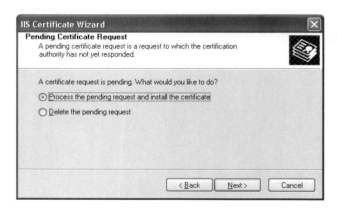

Figure 13.47
IIS Certificate Wizard Pending Certificate Request window.

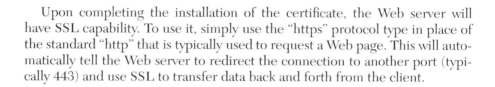

Upon completing the installation of the certificate, the Web server will have SSL capability. To use it, simply use the "https" protocol type in place of the standard "http" that is typically used to request a Web page. This will automatically tell the Web server to redirect the connection to another port (typically 443) and use SSL to transfer data back and forth from the client.

FTP Service

The File Transfer Protocol service is the most commonly used method of transferring large files across the Internet. Using the TCP/IP protocol, an FTP client makes a connection to an FTP host, which is also known as the FTP server. Once connected, the client can upload, download, and alter files on the FTP server as their permissions allow.

FTP is the transfer protocol of choice due to its ability to send files as binary. Other forms of data transfer, such as HTTP, can transfer large files. However, they transfer the file as ASCII, which can cause data corruption. Since this is such a popular tool, Microsoft included FTP in the Internet Information Services package.

To configure the FTP service, you will need to open the Internet Service Manager by clicking **Start ➤ Control Panel ➤ Administrative Tools ➤ Internet Information Services**. This will open a window similar to Figure 13.48.

The ISM, as previously discussed, is the control panel for the WWW and FTP services. In addition, it details the status of each of the services to keep administrators informed. In Figure 13.48, the FTP service is running on "All Unassigned" IP addresses at port 21. This is the typical default setup that you will see upon entering the ISM.

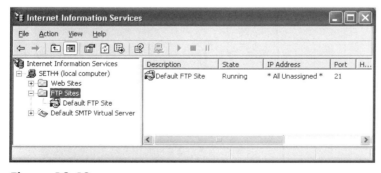

Figure 13.48
Internet Service Manager—FTP Sites.

Although other ports can be used, port 21 is the standard for the FTP service. Using a different port can provide a level of safety from random scanners, but it can also confuse clients attempting to connect with programs configured for the default port.

The following pages show you how to configure each of the FTP properties for maximum security.

Master FTP Site Properties

Control of the FTP service is layered. Just as in the WWW service, the FTP has a root folder that holds all the client sites. While there may be only one FTP site on the computer, the server can hold multiple sites for numerous clients or purposes. Each site may have its own properties and settings. However, to maintain the highest level of security, it is best to configure the root site at the highest security settings possible. Then, configure each individual site as needed.

The following describes how to configure the settings in each section to lock down the root site. Once we have covered the Master FTP Site Properties, we discuss the Default FTP Site Properties.

To access the Master FTP Site Properties sheet (Figure 13.49), right-click on **FTP Sites** and select **Properties.** Upon opening, you will see a window with three tabs: **Security Accounts**, **Messages**, and **Home Directory**.

Figure 13.49
Master FTP Site Properties—Security Accounts sheet.

Security Accounts Sheet

Allow Anonymous Connections. This section is used to control the anonymous user settings. Depending on the purpose of the FTP server, you may want to disable anonymous connections. By enabling anonymous connections, you allow someone to connect to your FTP server with the user name "anonymous" and an email address as the password, which can be easily forged. This is why you must ensure that any such sites created are done so with read-only permissions.

In addition to allowing anonymous connections, you can enable the server to accept ONLY anonymous connections. The reason for this is to avoid a situation where a user's name can be sniffed from the network. Due to the nature of FTP data transfer (i.e., clear text), it is best to avoid having users connect to the server with a user name and password. By enabling **Allow only anonymous connections**, the FTP server will reject any clients who connect with user information. Ironically, any user who is rejected has already sent their information and is subject to having their user info captured.

To ensure the anonymous FTP logon matches the account created by the server during install, keep **Allow IIS to control password** checked.

FTP Site Operators. The FTP Site Operators are those accounts that are used to administer the account. This should always consist of local accounts, as the computer the service is running on should not be included in any domain. If, however, the server is part of a network, you can use local, global, or universal accounts.

Messages Sheet

Banner/Welcome/Exit/Maximum connections. This sheet, shown in Figure 13.50, defines the messages the client will see when connecting to and exiting from the server. You may wish to include a legal disclaimer at this entry point.

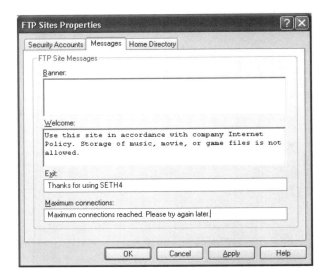

Figure 13.50
Master FTP Sites Properties—
Messages sheet.

Home Directory

FTP Site Directory. The FTP Site directory has three options you can select. However, by default the selection is secure. **Log visits** is the only box that should be checked. While enabling Read and Write may be acceptable for some situations, these should typically remain disabled. These options can be enabled at the Site level.

Directory Listing Style. The directory listing style is an option that is completely up to the Administrator. Since FTP originated within the UNIX operating system, some people are more comfortable with this style of listing than the MS-DOS style (Figure 13.51).

Figure 13.51
Master FTP Site Properties—Home
Directory sheet.

Default FTP Site Properties

Under the Master FTP Site folder you will find the specific FTP site information. You can create multiple sites for a host of users or purposes. If the Master FTP Sites configuration is correct, any new site should be locked down
upon creation, with the exception of Read properties.

The following discusses in detail the sections and their respective settings
for securing the FTP Server at the Site level.

FTP Site (Figure 13.52).

Identification. This section is used to configure several important options.
The first item in this section is the FTP site description. If there is only one
site, this option is not important. However, if the FTP server is destined to
host multiple sites, careful and descriptive labeling is important.

The second option is available in case there are multiple IP addresses
assigned to the server (e.g., an FTP site serving both the Internet and local
network). In this case, it may be necessary to permit only one IP address
access to the FTP site.

The final option in this section is the TCP port the FTP server will use as
the control port. This is the port with which clients will establish their initial connection. If the site is to be available to the general public, port 21 is

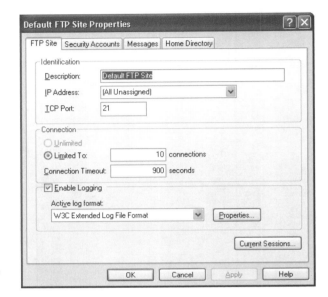

Figure 13.52
Default FTP Site Properties—FTP Site sheet.

recommended. However, if the site is to be private, moving the port can help protect the server against port-scanning hackers.

Connection. In order to protect the FTP server against a Denial of Service (DoS) situation, it is important to configure the site to limit both the number of connections and the timeout for inactive sessions. The default settings are adequate. However, if you are under consistent attack, you may wish to tighten these settings.

Enable Logging (Figure 13.53). This contains one of the most important settings for FTP administrators. An FTP server's log file is like a diary. It contains the address and actions of every user who connects or attempts to connect. If a log file is available after a hacker gains access to the server, it is possible to trace the activities of the hacker and repair or replace the files that were damaged.

By default, the settings for logging are correct, with the exception of the **Log file location**. If an experienced hacker gains access, the last thing she will delete or alter is the log file. If an FTP administrator hides the log file in an inconspicuous place, it makes it more difficult for the hacker to damage the logs. For this reason, we recommend the placement of the log file on another drive and, if possible, a different computer. To relocate the log file, click the **Properties** button and then click **Browse** to specify a new log file location.

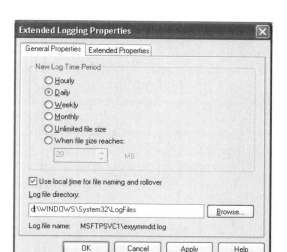

Figure 13.53
Extended Logging Properties.

In addition, the FTP server can be configured to capture supplementary information that can be useful when tracking traffic or troubleshooting a connection. This is also available in the log **Properties**, under the **Extended Properties** tab.

Current Sessions. The final section on this page is found by clicking the **Current Session** button. This opens a window, shown in Figure 13.54, that lets you view the current users, their IP address, and how long they have been connected. By monitoring this dialog box, you can keep track of the number of users and even disconnect someone if they are attempting multiple connections or if they are sharing accounts.

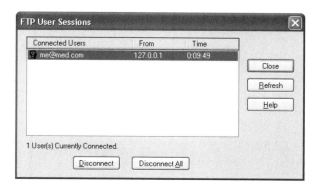

Figure 13.54
FTP User Session window.

Security Accounts

Allow Anonymous Connections. This section is used to control the anonymous user settings. Depending on the purpose of the FTP server, you may want to disable anonymous connections. However, you will typically allow anonymous connections. By doing so you allow someone to connect to your FTP server with the user name "Anonymous" and an email address as the password, which can be easily forged. This is why you must ensure that any sites created are done so with read-only permissions.

In addition to allowing anonymous connections, you can enable the server to accept ONLY anonymous connections. The reason for this is to avoid a situation where a user's name can be sniffed from the network. Due to the nature of FTP data transfer (i.e., clear text), it is best to avoid having users connect to the server with a user name and password. By enabling **Allow only anonymous connections**, the FTP server will reject any clients who connect with user information. Ironically, any user who is rejected has already sent their information and is subject to having their user info captured (Figure 13.55).

To ensure the anonymous FTP logon matches the account created by the server during install, keep **Allow IIS to control password** checked.

Figure 13.55
Default FTP Site Properties—Security Accounts sheet.

FTP Site Operators. The FTP Site Operators are those accounts that are used to administer the account. This should always consist of local accounts, as the computer the service is running on should not be included in any domain. If, however, the server is part of a network, you can use local, global, or universal accounts.

Messages

Banner/Welcome/Exit/Maximum connections. This sheet defines the messages the client will see when connecting and exiting the server. To help protect your system against misuse, it is suggested that you put a security warning or guidance policy in the Welcome message (Figure 13.56).

When a user connects to the FTP server they will see a message similar to that in Figure 13.57.

Figure 13.56
Default FTP Site Properties—Messages sheet.

Figure 13.57
Sample FTP Welcome message.

Home Directory (Figure 13.58).

Content Location. IIS includes a feature that enables a user to point any resource requests to a physical location on a remote computer. Using this feature can serve to protect a system by separating the requested resource from the FTP server. This prevents hackers from using folder-traversing vulnerabilities to gain access to the Internet system. However, this could allow one computer to access files on another computer.

FTP Site Directory. The FTP Site directory has three options you can select. However, by default the selection is secure. **Log visits** is the only box that should be checked. While enabling Read and Write may be acceptable for some situations, typically these should remain disabled. These options can be enabled at the Site level.

Directory Listing Style. The directory listing style is an option that is completely up to the Administrator. Since FTP originated within the UNIX operating system, some people are more comfortable with this style of listing than MS-DOS's style.

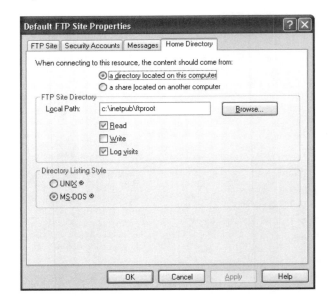

Figure 13.58
Default FTP Site Properties—Home Directory sheet.

Virtual FTP Directories

IIS FTP server allows the use of virtual directories. This simulates a hierarchal directory structure for the client, but in reality allows the directories to be located anywhere on the local computer or remote computer on the network. This setup would be useful if an FTP server had to span a cluster of servers, or if the FTP folder was mapped to a user's personal computer.

To create a virtual directory:

1. Open the ISM.
2. Right-click on the **Default FTP Site** folder.
3. Select **Properties** ➤ **New** ➤ **Virtual Directory** (see Figure 13.59).

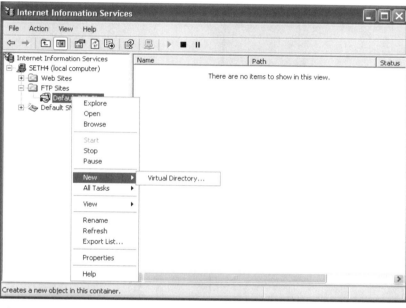

Figure 13.59
Starting the FTP Virtual Directory Creation Wizard.

4. Click **Next** at the Directory Creation Wizard welcome screen, shown in Figure 13.60.
5. Enter an Alias name and click **Next**. See Figure 13.61.

Figure 13.60
Directory Creation Wizard welcome screen.

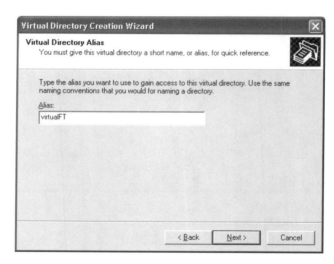

Figure 13.61
Virtual Directory Creation Wizard.

6. Click **Browse** to point the wizard to the desired path/folder (Figure 13.62).

7. Check either **Read** or **Write** as circumstances require. See Figure 13.63.

 Caution

You should not check both Read and Write. This allows a hacker to see what other people have placed in the directory and facilitates the unauthorized deletion or modification of previously uploaded files.

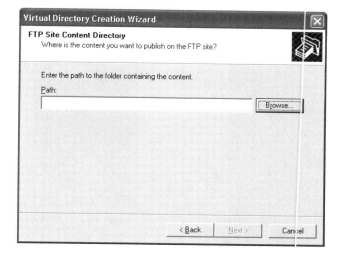

Figure 13.62
Virtual Directory Creation Wizard
(FTP Site Content Directory)

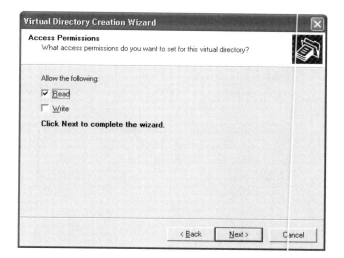

Figure 13.63
Virtual Directory Access Permission
configuration.

8. Click **Next** and then **Finish** to close the wizard.

Your new Virtual Directory is now set up. To view or modify the settings of the virtual directory, right-click the new directory and select **Properties**. This will open a window similar to Figure 13.64. From this window you can adjust the content location, local path, and directory permissions.

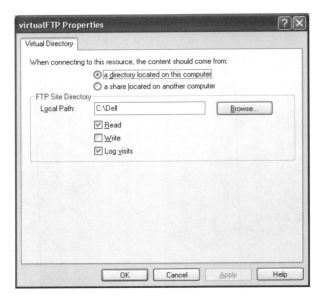

Figure 13.64
Virtual FTP Directory properties.

Exploit Scanners

Once you fully understand how to manually secure IIS, it never hurts to double-check your work. Fortunately, a new trend toward automated hardening tools such as exploit scanners is making this task easier. In this section we list the most popular tools to harden IIS and describe their advantages and disadvantages.

IIS Lockdown Tool

Microsoft has released *IIS Lockdown Wizard*, which provides templates for the major IIS-dependant Microsoft products. IIS Lockdown Wizard works by turning off unnecessary features, thereby reducing attack surface available to attackers. In addition, IIS Lockdown Wizard now integrates URLscan (described below), with customized templates for each supported server role.

To download IIS Lockdown Wizard, visit the following site: *www.microsoft.com/technet/security/tools/locktool.asp*.

URLScan Security Tool

Microsoft has also developed a tool that lets Web server administrators test the security of their servers. The tool, *URLScan*, screens all incoming requests to the server, and filters them based on rules set by the Administrator. This can potentially improve the security of the server by helping ensure that it only responds to valid requests.

URLScan works by helping to screen Web servers from unusual requests. For instance, an attack might consist of an extremely long request, a request for an unusual action, a request encoded using an alternate character set, or a request that includes character sequences that are rarely seen in legitimate requests. By filtering out unusual requests, URLScan can help prevent them from reaching the server and potentially causing damage.

To download URLScan, visit the following site: *www.microsoft.com/technet /security/tools/URLscan.asp.*

Although IIS Lockdown Wizard and URLScan are steps in the right direction, they are still baby steps. Microsoft has just started venturing into the esoteric world of information security, and they admit that they have a long way to go. For this reason, we also briefly mention the heavy artillery for network administrators who are fastidious about security.

Retina Network Security Scanner

Retina has won awards for being the best IIS exploit/vulnerability scanner on the market. The programmers at eEye Digital Security have been the technological leaders in this field for several years. Retina is easy to use, and it will quickly tune your Web server for maximum security against hackers.

Retina will scan your server, or a range of servers, for thousands of up-to-date exploits. Many of these exploits are brand new and are not available elsewhere. Retina also supports scheduled scanning. It outputs complete and extensive reports that are sure to impress your manager or CIO who, while not understanding it, can nevertheless show it to the board of directors as evidence of his security efforts (See Figure 13.65).

Retina can be downloaded at: *www.eeye.com.*

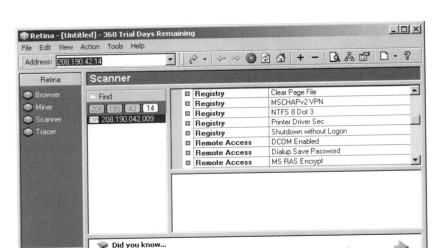

Figure 13.65
Retina.

SecureIIS Application Firewall

SecureIIS is another program from eEye Digital Security that can protect IIS from known and unknown attacks. SecureIIS wraps around IIS and works within it, verifying and analyzing incoming and outgoing data for possible security breaches. SecureIIS provides a level of both intrusion detection and Web server firewalling in one program, and it can be tuned to your individual Web server. SecureIIS is a useful tool that adds another layer of protection to your Web site.

SecureIIS can be downloaded at: *www.eeye.com.*

Summary

Windows .NET Server ships with an updated version of IIS. IIS is the single most hacked software application on the Internet. Nevertheless, thanks to enhanced features and security, IIS is growing in market share. By taking the time to configure IIS for security, you might save your company from unimaginable embarrassment and financial loss.

Chapter 14

CONFIGURING IP SECURITY

This chapter covers:

- Understanding IPSec
- Using the IPSec snap-in
- Configuring IPSec
- Enabling Audit Policy
- Using Network Monitor with IPSec
- Establishing an IPSec security plan

Overview

What Is IPSec?

IPSec is emerging as the most popular standard for securing data over a network. IPSec (short for *IP Security*) is a set of security standards designed by the Internet Engineering Task Force (IETF) to provide end-to-end protection of private data. Implementing this standard allows your enterprise to transport data across an untrustworthy network such as the Internet while preventing hackers from corrupting, stealing, or spoofing your communication. As part of a continuing effort by Microsoft Corporation to move toward industry security standards, Windows .NET Server makes IPSec easy (and even pleasurable) to configure.

By securing packets at the Network layer, IPSec provides application-transparent encryption services for IP network traffic as well as other access protections for secure networking. For example, IPSec can provide for end-to-end security from client-to-server, server-to-server, and client-to-client configurations using IPSec transport mode. IPSec also delivers machine-level authentication and encryption for VPNs based on the Layer 2 Tunneling Protocol. (Chapter 11 covers VPNs in detail.)

IPSec Protocols

IPSec is a suite of protocols that provides integrity protection, authentication, and optional privacy and replay protection services. The IPSec protocols encompass packet format, key exchange, and transforms that are defined by IETF RFCs 2401-2409.

The IPSec packets are comprised of the following types:

- IP Protocol 50: This is the **Encapsulating Security Payload** (ESP) format. It defines privacy, authenticity, and integrity.
- IP Protocol 51: This is the **Authentication Header** (AH) format. It defines authenticity and integrity, but not privacy.

IPSec Modes

IPSec operates in two modes, which are defined as follows:

Transport mode: In this mode, AH and ESP protect the transport payload. Transport mode defines point-to-point communication between source and destination computers.

Tunnel mode: IPSec is implemented in tunnel mode when the final destination of the packet differs from the security termination point. This mode is used when the security is provided by a device that did not originate the packets, such as in VPNs or router forwarding.

IPSec Encryption

The ESP protocol provides for data privacy using encryption. Under Windows .NET Server, IPSec utilizes encryption based on either DES (Data Encryption Standard), which is 56 bits, or 3DES (Triple DES), which is 3×56 or 168 bits in strength. Chapter 9 covers Windows .NET Server cryptographic services in more detail.

The beauty of the ESP and AH protocols is that they define an elegant framework for packet header formats and processing rules while leaving the transforms unspecified. Thus, the cryptographic algorithms can be updated as old algorithms become relatively weaker and less secure.

IPSec is a fascinating and complex subject that can form the basis of several books. The annotated bibliography in the Appendix of this book lists resources for readers who wish to learn more about the IPSec architecture and protocols. The rest of this chapter introduces the practical steps to configure IPSec on Windows .NET Server.

Why Use IPSec?

IPSec serves two purposes, which include the following:

1. Protecting the contents of IP packets
2. Defending against network attacks using packet filtering and trusted communication enforcement

The strength of IPSec is provided through the use of cryptography-based protection services, security protocols, and dynamic key management. This allows for end-to-end protection of communications between network components by establishing trust and security from a source IP to a destination IP address. For authentication purposes, either the IP address itself or the device using the IP address can prove identity. Only the computers at either end of the communication need to know identity, and communication can take place over an untrusted public network. This model allows IPSec to be deployed in various scenarios, including the following:

- Local area network (LAN)
- Wide area network (WAN)
- Dial-up clients and Internet access from private networks

Both ends of the communication must be configured to conform to a uniform *IPSec policy* (discussed below), including options and access controls that facilitate data transfer between two disparate systems. In Windows .NET Server, Group Policy can be utilized to deliver the IPSec configuration across the enterprise. Before designing your IP Security Policy, read the following sections to familiarize yourself with IPSec configuration in Windows .NET Server.

Using the IPSec Snap-in

In order to get started with IPSec configuration, the first step is to generate an IPSec MMC snap-in. For example, in order to set up an MMC for configuring IPSec on an individual machine, perform the following steps:

1. Click **Start ➤ Run** and type **mmc** in the console.
2. Click **Add/Remove Snap-in**.
3. In the **Add/Remove Snap-in** dialog box, click **Add**.
4. In the **Add Standalone Snap-in** dialog box, click **IP Security Management**, and then click **Add,** as shown in Figure 14.1.
5. Select **This Computer** and click **Finish**.
6. To close the **Add Standalone Snap-in** dialog box, click **Close**.
7. To close the **Add/Remove Snap-in** dialog box, click **OK**.

You now have an IPSec MMC for configuring security on the local machine. The next section details the steps for configuring IPSec.

Figure 14.1
Add Standalone Snap-in.

Configuring IPSec

Configuring IPSec policy (described below) involves choosing IP Security rules and then creating IP Filter lists and actions. IPSec can be configured for the local machine or can be integrated with Active Directory for a domain. From the IPSec Snap-In, perform the following steps to configure IPSec on the local machine:

1. Highlight **IP Security Policies on Local Machine.**
2. In the right pane, right-click **Secure Server** and select **Properties** from the drop-down menu, as shown in Figure 14.2.

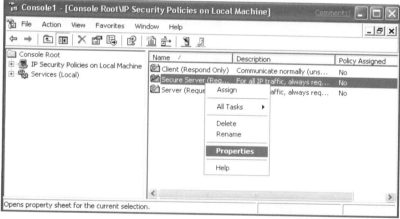

Figure 14.2
IPSec Console.

3. In the **Secure Server Properties** window, select the **Rules** tab.
4. Check the **Use Add Wizard** box in the lower right corner, as shown in Figure 14.3.

299

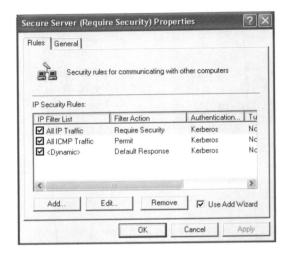

Figure 14.3
Secure Server (Require Security) Properties.

5. Click **Add**

6. Click **Next** on the **Security Rule Wizard**.

7. Select whether or not the rule specifies a tunnel and click **Next**. See Figure 14.4.

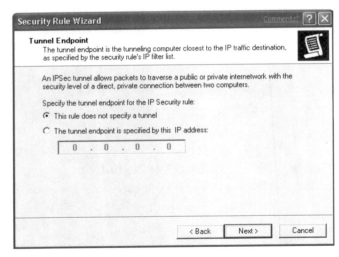

Figure 14.4
Security Rule Wizard (Tunnel Endpoint).

8. Select the Network Type. See Figure 14.5.

9. Select the **Authentication method** and click **Next.**

10. Select the **IP Filter Lists** and click **Next**. See Figure 14.6.

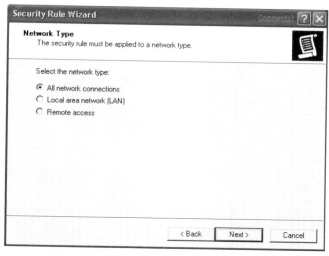

Figure 14.5
Security Rule Wizard (Network Type).

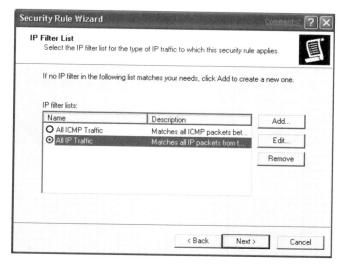

Figure 14.6
Security Rule Wizard (IP Filter List).

11. Select **Require Security** and click **Next.** See Figure 14.7.
12. Click **Finish** to close the Wizard.

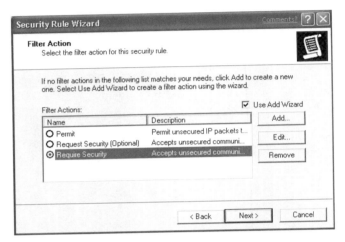

Figure 14.7
Security Rule Wizard (Filter Action).

Next, perform the following steps to assign the rule (Figure 14.8):

1. After you have completed the wizard, close the **Properties** box.

2. Select the **Secure Server Properties** and check the box of the rule you have just created.

3. In the right pane of the MMC Snap-in, select **Secure Server Properties** and click **Assign**.

Figure 14.8
Secure Server (Require Security)
Properties.

Enabling Audit Policy

This section shows you how to configure auditing in order to log events when IPSec is involved in communication.

To enable an audit policy, perform the following steps:

1. In the MMC, select **Local Computer Policy** from the left pane, shown in Figure 14.9, and expand to **Computer Configuration ➤ Windows Settings ➤ Security Settings ➤ Local Policies ➤ Audit Policy**.
2. In the right pane, double-click **Audit Logon Events**.
3. In the **Audit Logon Events** dialog box, select both the **Audit these attempts: Success and Failed** check boxes and click **OK**.
4. Repeat these steps for the **Audit Object Access** attribute.

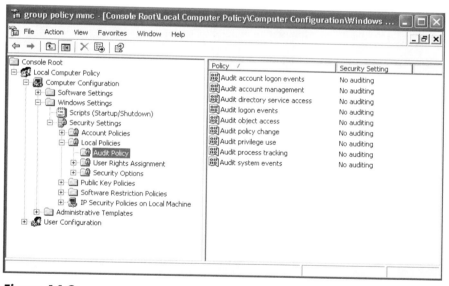

Figure 14.9
Group Policy MMC.

Using Network Monitor with IPSec

Windows .NET Server allows you to utilize the *Network Monitor* tool to view the IPSec security protocol transmissions. The Network Monitor captures information that has been transferred over a network at any given time.

In order to view IPSec packets, you will need to configure Network Monitor with the addresses of the source and destination computers for which you want to communicate. You can also assign the predefined IPSec policies and use the Ping tool to generate traffic to view with Network Monitor.

Network Monitor can display packets that are secured with AH as a TCP, ICMP, or UDP packet with an AH header. In the Next Header field, AH is displayed as IP protocol number 51 (in decimal).

In addition, Network monitor allows you to view ESP packets. However, the data payload in the ESP packet is encrypted. In the Next Header field, ESP is displayed as IP protocol number 50 (in decimal).

IPSec Statistics

In order to view IP security statistics, perform the following steps:

1. Open a console containing the IP Security Monitor.
2. Right-click a server name.
3. Click **Statistics,** as shown in Figure 14.10.

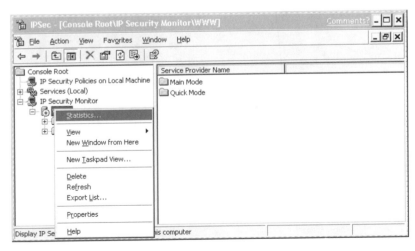

Figure 14.10
IPSec - [Console Root\IP Security Monitor\WWW].

304

Chapter 15

HOW TO BEAT BUGTRAQ BY SEVEN DAYS

This chapter covers:

- Cloaking your identity
- Maintaining anonymity
- Anonymous proxies
- Counterintelligence

Overview

Stalking the Hackers

As a network administrator, your job by default often includes keeping up with the latest vendor patches for security vulnerabilities. For an overworked and underpaid admin, the amount of effort required to stay current can be daunting. Nevertheless, we are constantly impressed by the valiant efforts of administrators who work overtime, without additional pay, to keep their networks secure from the latest hacker and virus threats.

Tip

You can outsource your network security monitoring to a Managed Security Provider such as VirusMD Corp. (www.VirusMD.com).

For those network admins who have a special interest in security and who enjoy staying ahead of the bell curve, we have included this chapter. In addition, this chapter will appeal to security consultants, law enforcement officers, and military experts who specialize in cybercrime.

Advanced users with an interest in security often subscribe to software vulnerability mailing lists such as Bugtraq. *Bugtraq* is the generic term for a large class of mailing lists that describe how to exploit (and how to fix) software applications by revealing their specific security weaknesses. There are currently several privately owned lists that use the name "Bugtraq." The majority of Bugtraq lists operate on the principle of *full disclosure*, which means that these weaknesses are announced publicly.

By keeping abreast of the most recently published exploits, you can often install patches on your system in time to prevent catastrophe. However, a list such as Bugtraq is limited in that it only lists *publicly known* vulnerabilities. In some situations, you may find that you also need access to *unknown* vulnerabilities as well. If this is the case, then your best source of knowledge is to go to the underground hackers themselves. Hackers often employ a technique known as *camping*, in which they keep an exploit secret for days until they can coordinate a massive strike. It is during this camped time, which is like the calm before the storm, that you can extract the occult data.

Disclaimer

Using the techniques described in this section, you will often be able to uncover the most dangerous vulnerabilities 7 days or more before they are exploited. However, counterintelligence (spying) on the hacker underground is a time-consuming and potentially dangerous endeavor. We do not recommend using the procedures in this chapter unless you are a law enforcement officer or working under the supervision of a law enforcement officer.

Examples of groups who might find it useful to have advance warning of vulnerabilities include the following sectors:

- Law Enforcement
- Government
- Military

- Infrastructure
- Finance
- Security Consultants
- Wargames Contestants (i.e., *www.dallascon.com*)

Before proceeding, it is important to pause and carefully consider ethics. If you do happen to come across a camped exploit, it is your ethical and legal duty to promptly notify both law enforcement and the manufacturer of the targeted software product. (The legal debate over posting vulnerabilities to full disclosure lists such as Bugtraq is beyond the scope of this book.)

Cloaking Your Identity

When traversing the computer underground, it is imperative to maintain anonymity. If a hacker detects that your IP address is coming from a .gov or .mil domain, he is unlikely to give up the crown jewels. Similarly, if you leave a trail you could expose yourself to retaliation. This section briefly describes how you can cloak yourself on the Internet.

Choosing an Alias

The most obvious step in masking your identity is to choose an alias, or fake screen name. A well-designed alias should engender trust in the hacker while providing no trace of its origin. As an example of a well-engineered alias, we will use the screen name "cornholio."

Using Anonymizers

When surfing the Internet, you leave a trail of information detritus that can be used to track you back to your workplace or home. Some of the information a hacker sees when you visit his Web site includes the following:

- *IP address*: The unique IP address that identifies you on the Internet. Your IP address is logged at almost every Web site and at the routers in between.
- *Browser type and operating system*: For example, "Mozilla/4.0 (compatible; MSIE 5.5; Windows 98)" is what your computer may reveal to Web

sites. This information is useful for a hacker to launch browser-based attacks against you.

- *Referrer*: The referrer is the Web site that "referred" or sent you to the Web site that is pulling this information from your computer. This means that your path or route to any Web site could be monitored, which might reveal clues to your identity.

All of the above information is what shows up even if you have the highest security settings on your computer. This is because your computer automatically sends every site it visits a description of itself. For example, your computer may be shouting out the following information:

```
Accept: image/gif, image/x-xbitmap, image/jpeg, image/pjpeg,
application/vnd.ms-powerpoint,         application/vnd.ms-excel,
application/msword, application/x-quickviewplus, */* Accept-
Language: en-us Connection: Keep-Alive Host: privacy.net
Referer:  http://www.anonymizer.com/why.shtml  User-Agent:
Mozilla/4.0 (compatible; MSIE 5.5; Windows 98) Accept-Encod-
ing: gzip, deflate
```

A quick way to cover your tracks is to use a Web-based anonymizing front end such as that found at *http://rewebber.de/* or at *http://anonymizer.com/*. However, such tools are limited and incomplete. In order to provide true anonymity, you will have to utilize anonymous proxies.

Anonymous Proxies

 Tip

For your convenience, we have included the software discussed in this chapter on the CD-ROM that accompanies this book.

MultiProxy

A correctly configured anonymous proxy can help give you complete anonymity. *http://multiproxy.org* offers proxy software as well as lists of anonymous proxies and excellent assistance in learning how to tune your system for anonymity.

As shown in Figure 15.1, MultiProxy listens on port 8088 by default, so you will need to configure your browser to connect to the Internet via a proxy server

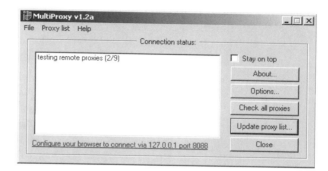

Figure 15.1
MultiProxy v1.2a.

at address 127.0.0.1 (localhost) and port 8088. You can change the port number from the Options dialog box. If you want other computers on your LAN (without Internet access) to connect to the Internet through MultiProxy, you need to enter the actual IP address of the computer where MultiProxy has been installed (instead of 127.0.0.1). You can quickly find your Internet-connected computer's IP address by running *ipconfig.exe* at a command prompt (console).

Configuring MultiProxy

Clicking the **Options** tab in MultiProxy reveals three tabs, as shown in Figure 15.2.

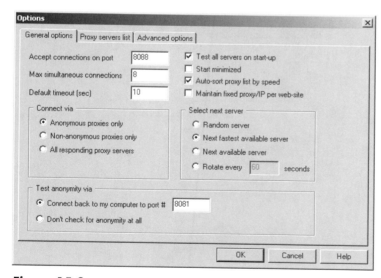

Figure 15.2
MultiProxy (General Options).

313

Under **General options**, select the following configuration:

- Accept connections on port: **8088**
- Connect via: **Anonymous Proxies Only**
- Connect back to my computer to port #: **8081**

You must next populate Multiproxy with a list of active anonymous proxies. Fortunately, *www.multiproxy.org* provides a fresh supply of regularly updated anonymous proxies.

Configuring Anonymous Browsing

Now that you have multiproxy configured, you must set your browser to utilize proxies. Depending on the browser type and version you are using, the settings will differ slightly.

Under your browser preferences, edit the "Proxies" information and make the following changes:

- In the **Address of proxy server to use**, for **HTTP** enter **127.0.0.1**, as shown in Figure 15.3.
- In the **Port** field, enter **8088.**

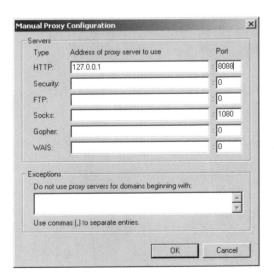

Figure 15.3
Manual Proxy Configuration.

Your browser is now configured for anonymous surfing.

Tip

Make sure to test your browser for anonymity before implementing it. Visit
http://privacy.net/ *for a quick online test of your anonymity.*

Configuring IRC for Anonymity

Without IRC (Internet Relay Chat), you will not get very far into the hacker
underground. IRC is the communication tool of choice for hackers.

Installing MIRC

MIRC is a popular client for using IRC. The latest version is available from
shareware download sites such as *www.download.com.*

After installing and starting MIRC, you will be able to connect to a hacker
IRC server (Figure 15.4).

Once you are connected you should see a welcome message. You can then
join a channel by typing **/join #channelname** at the prompt. Take care! You are
now conversing live with fearsome and elite hackers, as shown in Figure 15.5.

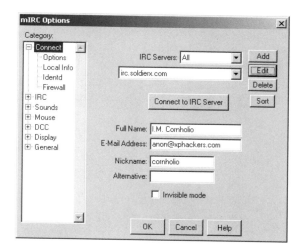

Figure 15.4
MIRC Options.

315

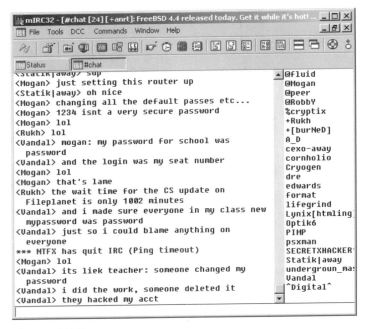

Figure 15.5
mIRC32.

We may think that our identity is now safe, but in fact we have made a glaring error. We are running multiproxy with anonymous servers, but everyone in the chat room easily read our IP address. In retaliation for our *faux pas* we can now expect to be DoS-ed, spammed, and Trojaned in every orifice of our network. How did this happen?

The answer lies in the fact that we need to integrate a SOCKS proxy to our HTTP anonymizer. The next segment shows you how to do this.

Socks2HTTP

Socks2HTTP is a software application that converts SOCKS v.5 requests into HTTP requests and tunnels them through an HTTP proxy. The SOCKS protocol allows programs to traverse firewalls on any port number and is used by many popular programs such as Napster, MSN Messenger, CRT (a Telnet client), and many others.

However, many network administrators restrict firewall traversals to HTTP requests only, thus disabling SOCKS proxies. Socks2HTTP allows users to circumvent this by providing a miniature SOCKS server for the SOCKS client, allowing it to perform its connection through an HTTP proxy. Thus, it is a very handy application. Unfortunately, later versions are embedded with adware, so unless you are lucky enough to have an older version, be prepared to deal with that drawback. You can find the latest version of Socks2HTTP at *www.totalrc.net*.

For our purposes, Socks2HTTP allows us to integrate MIRC with Multiproxy. To configure the applications, perform the following steps:

In Socks2HTTP

- Check the option **Try to detect proxy automatically**.
- In the field that says **SOCKS port**, enter **8088** (or whatever port you are using with Multiproxy).

In MIRC

- Open **Options** ➤ **Connect** ➤ **Firewall.**
- Check the **Use Firewall** box.
- For **Protocol**, check **Socks 5.**
- For **Hostname**, enter **127.0.0.1**.
- For **Port**, enter **8088**.

This is shown in Figure 15.6.

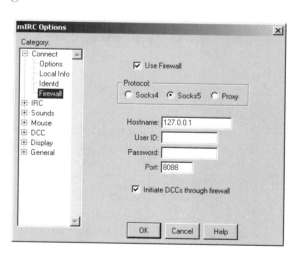

Figure 15.6
mIRC Firewall configuration.

You can now use IRC with total anonymity.

Tip

Using this configuration, you never have to worry about being banned from an IRC server again (or any server, for that matter). Simply spin Multiproxy to a new anonymous proxy, change your alias, and you will be able to circumvent the ban.

Counterintelligence

Once you have successfully masked your identity online, you can proceed to gather data. This is when a bit of social engineering skill comes in handy. If you show genuine interest and enthusiasm, many hackers will soon trust you enough to give up their precious custom exploits, which may be known to only a handful of people in the entire world.

True hackers are scholars, and as such they are drawn to other scholars. Thus, to gain credibility and respect you will also have to contribute research and development to their efforts. Keep in mind that many hackers score in the 99.9 percentile of standardized intelligence tests, so when they meet a kindred intellect they will embrace it.

 Caution

Make sure to get permission from the U.S. government export control agency (BXA), and other pertinent agencies, before exporting technology outside of the United States.

 Caution

Due to recent hysteria surrounding cyberattacks, Congress has passed legislation making it an offense, punishable by life imprisonment without parole, to give advice to hackers. Make sure to consult with legal counsel before taking any action described in this chapter.

A more advanced technique is to perform your own defacements on authorized sites, that is, perform cleverly faked attacks on networks that you secretly have (written) permission to legally penetrate. The FBI recently used this tactic to successfully infiltrate a number of hacker groups over a six-month period.

Summary

By using the techniques in this chapter with skill and perseverance, you will soon find that you have access to exploits far in advance of public knowledge. Using systemized infiltration, within a short period you can develop a sophisticated, global network of security intelligence.

In closing, there are a few words of caution to keep in mind. Remember that these techniques are dangerous and should be supervised by trained law enforcement organizations. In addition, if you do happen to come across camped exploits, make sure to promptly report them to the proper authorities. Finally, it is tempting to dismiss young hackers as "script kiddies," but keep in mind that these hackers are just like the ones that reportedly have penetrated the United States Central Intelligence Agency (CIA) and other highly secure networks. For example, one hacking group with an estimated average member age of 16 defaced nearly 100 *security consulting* Web sites in the same day. In fact, according to attrition.org, one Web site with its own Bugtraq was itself defeated: Security Focus had its banner advertisements indirectly replaced for several hours by a group of young hackers known as Fluffi Bunni. This group, whose mascot is a stuffed pink rabbit, jokingly altered the site banner advertisements from "Security Focus" to "Security Fluffi" (Figure 15.7). Fortunately, by applying the simple counterintelligence techniques outlined in this chapter, such embarrassing compromises can often be easily prevented.

Figure 15.7
Fluffi Bunni.

You think you know ? You have no idea..
- security fluffi

 Tip

To learn more secrets from the hacker underground, read our book Windows Internet Security: Protecting Your Critical Data *(Prentice-Hall PTR, 2002, ISBN 0130428310), by Seth Fogie and Cyrus Peikari.*

SUGGESTED READING

 Tip

Some of these suggestions are hyperlinks (URLs) on the World Wide Web. By nature, these links are transient. You can always obtain current recommendations by contacting the authors directly. If there is a reference that you think should be here, please contact the authors for possible inclusion in the next edition of this book.

Cyrus Peikari: cyrus@virusmd.com
Seth Fogie: seth@virusmd.com

On the Web

www.Dallascon.com—The largest security conference in the Southwest; includes mini-courses and certification in computer security.

www.virusmd.com—Expert security consultants.

www.securitynewsportal.com—SNP is the leading source for security news online.

http://microsoft.com/security—Get Windows .NET security updates from the source itself.

http://nsa.gov—Let the friendly folks at the NSA help you secure your Windows servers through their excellent resource guides online.

www.InformIT.com—Fresh columns from leading IT and security authorities.

www.zor.org—Maintains a master list of spyware, backdoors, and programs that phone home.

www.EFF.org—Protecting your security and Constitutional rights online. The EFF was instrumental in defending security researcher Dmitry Sklyarov.

www.eeye.com—Advanced software tools to help lock down your Windows XP networks.

www.robertgraham.com—A comprehensive security lexicon from one of the world's foremost security experts.

www.vmyths.com—a refreshing study of computer viruses.

Newsgroup: **microsoft.public.windowsxp.security_admin**: A Microsoft newsgroup focused exclusively on Windows XP security for admins. Join us there to get help and to help others in return.

Books

At the time of this writing, there are no other printed references on Windows .NET Server Security—this book is the first. However, the following are recommended texts for gaining a broader understanding of security on the Windows platform.

Fogie, Seth, and Cyrus Peikari. *Windows Internet Security: Protecting Your Critical Data.* Prentice Hall PTR, 2002. Our first book explains how hackers attack your network and how to protect your privacy online.

Ford, Warwick, and Michael S. Baum. *Secure Electronic Commerce: Building the Infrastructure for Digital Signatures and Encryption, 2E.* Prentice Hall PTR, 2001. The classic masterpiece of PKI. Highly recommended.

Pelmutter, Bruce, and Jonathan Zarkower. *Virtual Private Networking: A View from the Trenches.* Prentice Hall PTR, 2000. An excellent reference for a deeper understanding of VPNs.

Doraswamy, Naganand, and Dan Harkins. *IPSec: The new Security Standard for the Internet, Intranets, and Virtual Private Networks.* Prentice Hall

PTR, 1999. An excellent reference text for understanding IPSec in detail.

Fortenberry, Thaddeus. *Windows 2000 Virtual Private Networking*. New Riders, 2001. A must-read for anyone planning to deploy Windows-based VPNs.

Shinder, Tom. *Configuring ISA Server 2000*. Syngress, 2001. Learn to use ISA Server to protect your network. Dr. Shinder is a fellow medical doctor in Dallas who is also an expert in Internet security.

Norberg, Stefan. *Securing Windows NT/2000 Servers for the Internet*. O'Reilley, 2000. Excellent text on how to strip down a Windows machine by removing unnecessary services.

McLean, Ian. *Windows 2000 Security Little Black Book*. Coriolis, 2000. An efficient guidebook to locking down Windows 2000 Servers.

Cox, Philip, and Tom Sheldon. *Windows 2000 Security Handbook*. Osborne, 2001. Another excellent guide to Windows 2000.

Schmidt, Jeff. *Windows 2000 Security Handbook*. Que, 2000. Read this classic Windows security text from cover to cover. Highly recommended.

INDEX

R

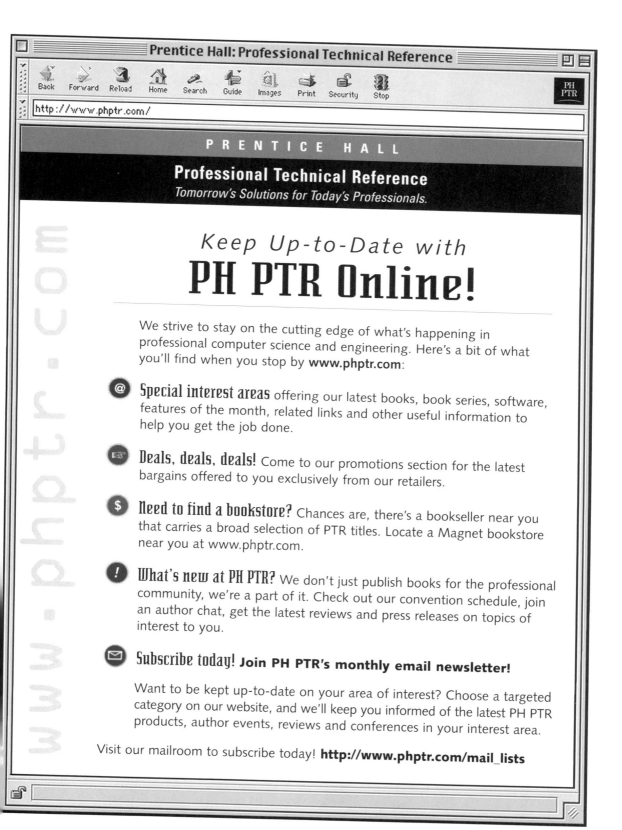

LICENSE AGREEMENT AND LIMITED WARRANTY

READ THE FOLLOWING TERMS AND CONDITIONS CAREFULLY BEFORE OPENING THIS SOFTWARE PACKAGE. THIS LEGAL DOCUMENT IS AN AGREEMENT BETWEEN YOU AND PRENTICE-HALL, INC. (THE "COMPANY"). BY OPENING THIS SEALED SOFTWARE PACKAGE, YOU ARE AGREEING TO BE BOUND BY THESE TERMS AND CONDITIONS. IF YOU DO NOT AGREE WITH THESE TERMS AND CONDITIONS, DO NOT OPEN THE SOFTWARE PACKAGE. PROMPTLY RETURN THE UNOPENED SOFTWARE PACKAGE AND ALL ACCOMPANYING ITEMS TO THE PLACE YOU OBTAINED THEM FOR A FULL REFUND OF ANY SUMS YOU HAVE PAID.

1. **GRANT OF LICENSE:** In consideration of your payment of the license fee, which is part of the price you paid for this product, and your agreement to abide by the terms and conditions of this Agreement, the Company grants to you a nonexclusive right to use and display the copy of the enclosed software program (hereinafter the "software") on a single computer (i.e., with a single CPU) at a single location so long as you comply with the terms of this Agreement. The Company reserves all rights not expressly granted to you under this Agreement.

2. **OWNERSHIP OF SOFTWARE:** You own only the magnetic or physical media (the enclosed software) on which the software is recorded or fixed, but the Company retains all the rights, title, and ownership to the software recorded on the original software copy(ies) and all subsequent copies of the software, regardless of the form or media on which the original or other copies may exist. This license is not a sale of the original software or any copy to you.

3. **COPY RESTRICTIONS:** This software and the accompanying printed materials and user manual (the "Documentation") are the subject of copyright. You may <u>not</u> copy the Documentation or the software, except that you may make a single copy of the software for backup or archival purposes only. You may be held legally responsible for any copying or copyright infringement which is caused or encouraged by your failure to abide by the terms of this restriction.

4. **USE RESTRICTIONS:** You may <u>not</u> network the software or otherwise use it on more than one computer or computer terminal at the same time. You may physically transfer the software from one computer to another provided that the software is used on only one computer at a time. You may <u>not</u> distribute copies of the software or Documentation to others. You may <u>not</u> reverse engineer, disassemble, decompile, modify, adapt, translate, or create derivative works based on the software or the Documentation without the prior written consent of the Company.

5. **TRANSFER RESTRICTIONS:** The enclosed software is licensed only to you and may <u>not</u> be transferred to any one else without the prior written consent of the Company. Any unauthorized transfer of the software shall result in the immediate termination of this Agreement.

6. **TERMINATION:** This license is effective until terminated. This license will terminate automatically without notice from the Company and become null and void if you fail to comply with any provisions or limitations of this license. Upon termination, you shall destroy the Documentation and all copies of the software. All provisions of this Agreement as to warranties, limitation of liability, remedies or damages, and our ownership rights shall survive termination.

7. **MISCELLANEOUS:** This Agreement shall be construed in accordance with the laws of the United States of America and the State of New York and shall benefit the Company, its affiliates, and assignees.

8. **LIMITED WARRANTY AND DISCLAIMER OF WARRANTY:** The Company warrants that the software, when properly used in accordance with the Documentation, will operate in substantial conformity with the description of the software set forth in the Documentation. The Company does not warrant that the software will meet your requirements or that the operation of the software will be uninterrupted or error-free. The Company warrants that the media on which the software is delivered shall be free from defects in materials and workmanship under normal use

for a period of thirty (30) days from the date of your purchase. Your only remedy and the Company's only obligation under these limited warranties is, at the Company's option, return of the warranted item for a refund of any amounts paid by you or replacement of the item. Any replacement of software or media under the warranties shall not extend the original warranty period. The limited warranty set forth above shall not apply to any software which the Company determines in good faith has been subject to misuse, neglect, improper installation, repair, alteration, or damage by you. EXCEPT FOR THE EXPRESSED WARRANTIES SET FORTH ABOVE, THE COMPANY DISCLAIMS ALL WARRANTIES, EXPRESS OR IMPLIED, INCLUDING WITHOUT LIMITATION, THE IMPLIED WARRANTIES OF MERCHANTABILITY AND FITNESS FOR A PARTICULAR PURPOSE. EXCEPT FOR THE EXPRESS WARRANTY SET FORTH ABOVE, THE COMPANY DOES NOT WARRANT, GUARANTEE, OR MAKE ANY REPRESENTATION REGARDING THE USE OR THE RESULTS OF THE USE OF THE SOFTWARE IN TERMS OF ITS CORRECTNESS, ACCURACY, RELIABILITY, CURRENTNESS, OR OTHERWISE.

IN NO EVENT, SHALL THE COMPANY OR ITS EMPLOYEES, AGENTS, SUPPLIERS, OR CONTRACTORS BE LIABLE FOR ANY INCIDENTAL, INDIRECT, SPECIAL, OR CONSEQUENTIAL DAMAGES ARISING OUT OF OR IN CONNECTION WITH THE LICENSE GRANTED UNDER THIS AGREEMENT, OR FOR LOSS OF USE, LOSS OF DATA, LOSS OF INCOME OR PROFIT, OR OTHER LOSSES, SUSTAINED AS A RESULT OF INJURY TO ANY PERSON, OR LOSS OF OR DAMAGE TO PROPERTY, OR CLAIMS OF THIRD PARTIES, EVEN IF THE COMPANY OR AN AUTHORIZED REPRESENTATIVE OF THE COMPANY HAS BEEN ADVISED OF THE POSSIBILITY OF SUCH DAMAGES. IN NO EVENT SHALL LIABILITY OF THE COMPANY FOR DAMAGES WITH RESPECT TO THE SOFTWARE EXCEED THE AMOUNTS ACTUALLY PAID BY YOU, IF ANY, FOR THE SOFTWARE.
SOME JURISDICTIONS DO NOT ALLOW THE LIMITATION OF IMPLIED WARRANTIES OR LIABILITY FOR INCIDENTAL, INDIRECT, SPECIAL, OR CONSEQUENTIAL DAMAGES, SO THE ABOVE LIMITATIONS MAY NOT ALWAYS APPLY. THE WARRANTIES IN THIS AGREEMENT GIVE YOU SPECIFIC LEGAL RIGHTS AND YOU MAY ALSO HAVE OTHER RIGHTS WHICH VARY IN ACCORDANCE WITH LOCAL LAW.

ACKNOWLEDGMENT

YOU ACKNOWLEDGE THAT YOU HAVE READ THIS AGREEMENT, UNDERSTAND IT, AND AGREE TO BE BOUND BY ITS TERMS AND CONDITIONS. YOU ALSO AGREE THAT THIS AGREEMENT IS THE COMPLETE AND EXCLUSIVE STATEMENT OF THE AGREEMENT BETWEEN YOU AND THE COMPANY AND SUPERSEDES ALL PROPOSALS OR PRIOR AGREEMENTS, ORAL, OR WRITTEN, AND ANY OTHER COMMUNICATIONS BETWEEN YOU AND THE COMPANY OR ANY REPRESENTATIVE OF THE COMPANY RELATING TO THE SUBJECT MATTER OF THIS AGREEMENT.

Should you have any questions concerning this Agreement or if you wish to contact the Company for any reason, please contact in writing at the address below.

Robin Short
Prentice Hall PTR
One Lake Street
Upper Saddle River, New Jersey 07458

ABOUT THE CD-ROM

The CD-ROM included with *Windows® .NET Server Security Handbook* contains the following:

- VirusMD Anti-Trojan Firewall
  VirusMD Personal Firewall 3.0 is an intelligent utility to help experts in the diagnosis and treatment of Trojan horse infections.
- eEye exploit scanner demo
  Retina is the award winning network vulnerability scanner that discovers and helps fix all known security vulnerabilities on internet, intranet, and extranet systems.
- eEye IDS demo
  SecureIIS protects Microsoft IIS (Internet Information Services) Web servers from known and unknown attacks.
- eEye sniffer demo
  A next-generation network protocol analyzer or "sniffer," Iris allows the network administrator to capture and retrace the steps of any network user with never-before-seen ease.
- LC3 Password tester
  LC3 helps administrators secure Windows-authenticated networks through comprehensive auditing of Windows NT and Windows 2000 user account passwords.
- MIRC
  mIRC is a configurable IRC client that has an intuitive user interface, an events handler, and full send-and-receive capabilities for DCC (direct client connection) files (see screenshot).
- Multi Proxy
  MultiProxy listens on port 8088 by default, so you will need to configure your browser to connect to Internet via proxy server at address 127.0.0.1 (localhost) and port 8088.
- Socks 2 http
  Socks2HTTP is a software application that converts SOCKS v.5 requests into HTTP requests and tunnels them through an HTTP proxy.
- NS wireless security tester
  NetStumbler sets the standard for wireless network scanning tools. NetStumbler ties into a local wireless network card and turns the host computer into a sniffer for wireless networks.

The CD-ROM can be used on Microsoft Windows® 95/98/NT®/2000/XP/.NET.

License Agreement

Use of the software accompanying *Windows® .NET Server Security Handbook* is subject to the terms of the License Agreement and Limited Warranty, found on the previous two pages.

Technical Support

Prentice Hall does not offer technical support for any of the programs on the CD-ROM. However, if the CD-ROM is damaged, you may obtain a replacement copy by sending an email that describes the problem to: disc_exchange@prenhall.com.